YEMEN

Traditionalism
vs.
Modernity

Mohammed Ahmad Zabarah

PRAEGER SPECIAL STUDIES • PRAEGER SCIENTIFIC

Library of Congress Cataloging in Publication Data

Zabarah, Mohammed Ahmad.
    Yemen, traditionalism vs. modernity.

    Bibliography: p.
    Includes index.
    1. Yemen—Politics and government. I. Title.
DS247.Y48Z3   953'.32   81-20982
ISBN 0-03-060081-2   AACR2

Dedicated to my

Father and Mother

Published in 1982 by Praeger Publishers
CBS Educational and Professional Publishing
a Division of CBS Inc.
521 Fifth Avenue, New York, New York 10175 U.S.A.

23456789   145   987654321

Printed in the United States of America

ACKNOWLEDGMENTS

It is with deep humility and respect that I extend my thanks and appreciation to Professor Muhammad Mughissuddin, dean of International Programs at the American University, who encouraged me to publish this work. I also would like to express my fond appreciation to the prime minister of the Yemen Arab Republic, Dr. Abdul Karim al-Iryani, for the honor he bestowed on me by granting me an interview. Special thanks are also extended to Abdullah al-Kurshimi, minister of Labor and Works, for his efforts to explain to me the projects undertaken by his ministry. His cooperation and assistance will always be appreciated. My gratitude is also extended to Ali Luft al-Thawr, Yemen's foreign minister, for his replies to my inquiries.

Special thanks I extend to my friends Ibrahim Ali al-Wazir; Yahya al-Mutawakkil, ambassador of Yemen to the United States; Ibrahim M. al-Kibsi, deputy foreign minister; Abdullah Sharafi, director of the Council of State; Ali Abdullah Ali, economic advisor to the Central Planning Organization; Dr. Abdul Wahid al-Zindani, director of Sanaa University; and Mohammed Motahar, vice-director of Sanaa University. Their advice and brotherly interest in this endeavor will always be remembered with fondness.

My thanks are extended to Diane Ponasik, Agency for International Development project officer in Yemen, for her professional advice and assistance. To James Callahan, cultural officer of the American embassy in Sanaa, I am greatly indebted for his help and support.

Special thanks are due to Jane Shepherd and Bobbi Davis for their work in getting this book ready.

Finally, I express my love and appreciation to my father, who took special interest in the formulation of this work and who had to go through a great deal of inconvenience.

Mohammed Ahmad Zabarah
Washington, D.C.
August 1981

CONTENTS

INTRODUCTION

PURPOSE

The purpose of this book is to describe, analyze, and evaluate the forces that produced a changing political, social, and economic order in Yemen. The descriptive method is used to review and examine the development of political institutions in Yemen and to evaluate the sociopolitical system of the state. The analytical method serves to illustrate changes in the affairs of Yemen, internally and externally.

This book purports to examine the effects internal conflicts and external penetrations have had in altering Yemen from a traditionalist society into a revolutionary state. Two objectives are closely followed in this book. The first is an examination of the imamic regime from 1918 until its demise in 1962. The evaluation concentrates on contradictions within the political and social order and examines their effects on the polity. The second objective concentrates on evaluating the revolutionary era, 1962-69, and the external intervention that followed the Revolution. In general, this book focuses on the rivalry between traditionalism and modernism in Yemen.

The study is divided into four periods: the isolationist era of pre-1948, the transitional era of the reign of Imam Ahmad, the revolutionary and civil war period, and the era of national growth. The pre-1948 era is examined in terms of the historical factors that influenced the imamic regime to adopt a strict isolationist policy. The focus of the discussion is on the regime's inability to maintain an equilibrium between its desire to remain isolationist and its wish to import modern technology. The regime's failure to resolve this particular problem is shown to result in the evolution of dissident movements and in the rise of internal conflicts.

Regarding the era of transition (1948-62), the focus is on the impact of the influx of modern ideas into Yemen as generated by Arab nationalism, the issues of reform and succession, and the 1955 coup d'etat. The inconsistencies of the Yemeni regime during this era are evaluated as is the rivalry between traditionalism and modernism.

The civil war era (1962-69) was a period of violence and intra-Arab involvement. Big power interests in Yemen were also manifest during this period. The focus is on the effects of the Yemeni Revolution regionally and internationally. This period witnessed the neutralism of traditionalism in Yemen as a unified resistance movement.

The fourth part focuses its attention on the Yemen Arab Republic in its attempts toward national growth. It evaluates the country's socioeconomic and political changes. The book concludes by examining the effects modern changes have had on traditionalism in the Yemen Arab Republic and what new contradictions have arisen as a consequence of those changes.

REVIEW OF SOURCES

Yemen's isolationism from 1918 until 1948 negatively affected the availability of literature on the country to Western and Arab writers. From 1918, the year of independence from Turkish rule, until 1948 Yemen was almost inaccessible to foreign interests and foreign personnel. Only a handful of Europeans were able to enter Yemen and write narratives about their experiences. Such narratives were essentially descriptive and nonpolitical. Yemen became more accessible after 1948. The regime's fears and apprehensions of anything foreign remained a barrier to outsiders. Nonetheless, foreign investments and companies were permitted to do business in the country, albeit under strict regulations.

Prior to 1948, practically all English writings on Yemen were either descriptive or historical in nature. Only after 1960, and specifically after the Revolution of 1962, is one able to locate literature that politically analyzes Yemen's policy and international position. The writer has been able to locate only two such books in English on Yemen dating to pre-1948. Stanley Trelton, The Rise of the Imams in Sana (London: H. Milford, Oxford University Press, 1925) and H. Fenton Jacob, The Kingdom of Yemen: Its Place in the Comity of Nations (London: 1933). Both are relatively outmoded and essentially historical. Recent Western scholarly work on Yemen includes Manfred Wenner, Modern Yemen: 1918-1966 (Baltimore: Johns Hopkins University Press, 1967), a political history of the period 1918-66; Kathryn Boals, Modernization and Intervention: Yemen as a Theoretical Case Study (Ph.D. dissertation, Princeton University, 1970), which uses Yemen as a case study in an inquiry into the relationship between intervention and modernization; and Robert Stookey, Political Change in Yemen: A Study of Values and Legitimacy (Ph.D. dissertation, University of Texas at Austin, 1972). These works have contributed greatly to promoting the study of Yemen. In general, all of these works tend to be subjective, highly cosmetic in their analyses, and partial in their treatments of the subject matter. Specifically, they incorrectly emphasized the significance of the internal or the external factors that promoted political change in Yemen as opposed to this more conclusive analysis.

The Revolution of 1962 in Yemen aroused the intellectual curiosity of the West. Many journalists, such as Dana Adams Schmidt,[1] who witnessed the civil war firsthand, have written narratives about it and the Yemeni society. Although these journalists have contributed more published data on Yemen, students of Yemen still face a serious problem in locating scholarly material. For this reason, the writer contacted several highly distinguished Yemenis who have contributed in their various capacities to the political development of the country. Those chosen for personal and/or written interviews were selected because they represented the broad spectrum of political views in Yemen. Each individual was sent a questionnaire, and personal interviews were held with five of the six respondents— Abdul Karim Al-Iriani, prime minister of the Yemen Arab Republic; Ali Luft Al-Thawr, foreign minister of Yemen; Ahmad Zabarah, former minister of state and chargé d'affaires of the legation of the Mutawakkilite Kingdom of Yemen to the United States; Ibrahim Al-Kibsi, deputy foreign minister; and Abdullah al-Kurshomi, minister of Labor and Works. A formal reply was received by the writer from Ibrahim al-Wazir outlining the political program of the Yemini Popular Forces Union. The questions asked were designed to provide data relative to the factors that brought about political change and national growth in Yemen. The writer was also involved in conversations with members of the embassy of the Yemen Arab Republic in Washington, D.C. and with high Yemeni dignitaries in Yemen.

Unlike the English sources, Arabic references on Yemen are voluminous. They do tend to be overly descriptive and historical. Nonetheless, they are valuable in that they offer the reader a point of view different from that presented in English works. A great many of the Arabic sources on the imamate regime tend to be highly critical and subjective. The writer attempted to use only those materials containing a certain degree of objectivity. Writers unjustly critical of the imamate are regarded as critics in the context of this book.

The scarcity of scholarly and academic work on Yemen hinders a comprehensive examination of an area rich in history and culture. Students of Yemen need to enliven scholarly interests in the country. To understand is to be sympathetic. If this book succeeds in contributing to the development of future studies on Yemen, it will have served one of its objectives.

ORIENTATION AND METHODOLOGY

The element that distinguishes this book from those previously cited and from others is that it identifies and analyzes the forces of internal conflicts and external penetrations as the forces most responsible for the move toward the formation of a new political order in the form of the Yemen Arab Republic. It is the contention of this writer that the internal conflicts in Yemen would not have been sufficient to alter the political and social environment without the help of the external entity. Internal conflicts went hand in hand with external penetrations in influencing political change.

To study Yemen's political development and to understand the effects internal conflicts and external penetrations have had on the Yemeni polity, a typology of the Yemeni political system under the imamate rule is formulated so that an appreciation of the Yemeni political system can be obtained. However, it is necessary to suspend momentarily the formulation of a typology in order to discuss the methodological approaches used in the book.

The three methods employed to accomplish the objectives of this book are the historical, the analytical, and the comparative.

The historical approach is used to review the Yemeni society during the imamate era (1918-48) and to identify the sociopolitical institutions of the polity. It examines the policy decisions of the regimes and evaluates their effects on the sociopolitical systems. It is hoped that some light will be shed on the process and development of the rise of dissident movements.

The second approach is used because of its intrinsic value to the study of political change in Yemen. The theoretical concept of coherency and incoherency and the hypotheses on polarity encounters as developed by Manfred Halpern serve as the framework for this study.[2] The analysis also evaluates the ideological conflicts between traditionalism and modernism in the Arab world and their significance to the political development of Yemen.

The comparative approach is used to illustrate the basic differences and similarities between the coups d'etat of 1948 and 1955 and the Revolution of 1962. In this approach, the fundamental analysis reflects on the principles of revolution and coup d'etat. Toward this objective, Karl Deutsch's concept of revolution and coup d'etat is applied. Deutsch asserts that "violent transformation involving a large part of society is called <u>revolution</u>, as distinct from <u>coup d'etat</u> or palace revolution, which merely change the people in power or a few laws, without changes in the fundamentals of social living."[3]

David Apter in his book, <u>The Politics of Modernization,</u> classifies political systems as either oriented toward a secular-libertarian or sacred-collectivity model. The former possesses the capacity to reason and to know self-interest.[4] This model permits the interplay of ideas, avoids the monopoly of power, encourages the equality of its citizens under the law, and maintains a close watch over those exercising power by legal means, such as the "checks and balances" found in the U.S. federal system.[5] The individual in such a model is conceived of as a free entity whose rights and liberties are guaranteed by laws. The sacred-collectivity framework, on the other hand, includes all traditional and theocratic systems and certain modernizing ones as well.[6] This model is considered the key to social life,[7] with the individual "merely a derivative, a derived personality."[8] The sacred-collectivity system is an ethical community within which the individual depends on the morality of the system. The adherence to higher laws (kinship, clan, religion) is basic in such a system. The sacred-collectivity model assumes that whatever is good for the community is good for the individual. The individual is bound by higher laws to uphold the good of the community above all else, and thus personal liberties and rights must be subordinated. This further ensures that innovations that contradict the polity will be rejected to maintain the continuity of traditional values.

The Mutawakkilite Kingdom of Yemen (imamate) on which this book concentrates can be modeled as a sacred-collectivity system. The term "Mutawakkilite" evokes religion. Specifically, it means "under the guidance of Allah." The rulers of the kingdom were referred to as imams, hence the term imamate. An imam is a religiopolitical leader who is granted by Islamic law, <u>Shari'a</u>, supreme authority in spiritual and civil matters. The sacredness of the state was apparent in the title adopted by Imam Yahya and Imam Ahmad. Both were referred to as <u>Amir al-Mu'mineen</u>, "Commander of the Faithful," which symbolized the theoretical permanence of the state and the Islamic community. The legitimacy of the political system was founded on Islamic grounds, and, as such, traditionalism was the cornerstone of the polity.

In a sacred-collectivity system, the ruler, who by traditional or religious beliefs is given absolute or nearly absolute power, usually must be a person of higher qualities unless the right of descent is hereditary. In such a case, the qualities of the individual are of secondary importance. In all traditional societies, the ruler must adhere to the nomos, the basic values and beliefs cherished by the polity. According to Plato, rulers are just if they observe the nomos, but unjust if they do not. [9] In this sense, justice is the adherence to traditional precepts and beliefs. Adherence to the nomos gives the ruler legitimacy, and legitimacy is granted by the people to a ruler when they believe him to have a right to rule. By adhering to the nomos, the ruler solidifies his legitimacy, enhances stability, and gains public support for his policy decisions. Violations of traditional values by a ruler weaken his claim to legitimacy but not his power to authoritatively allocate goals. Nonetheless, violations of traditional beliefs weaken the political institutions and endanger the longevity of the political order.

In a sacred-collectivity system, authoritatively allocated goals are usually derived through either a hierarchical or a segmented political structure. The hierarchical structure is one in which the ruler is the apex of the political system. He is the central figure who makes essential choices. Loyalty to the ruler is expected. Subordinates who fail in their loyalty to their leader are subject to removal and castigation. The ruler becomes the central figure in the political system, if not the polity. He presides over the entire society as a parent presides over a household. Nothing is done without the expressed approval of the ruler. The system rotates around the central figure of the leader.

A segmented structure presupposes that there are no fixed institutions through which decisions are authoritatively made. Instead, ad hoc coalitions are created and dismantled whenever circumstances dictate. Primitive societies based on kinship linkage contain a high degree of segmented authority.

The imamate regime in Yemen was a hierarchical system. The imams were able to subordinate tribal values to Zeidi laws. (Zeidism is a religiopolitical doctrine of Islam.) However, the imams' violations of Zeidi precepts weakened the political structure and their legitimacy. Their abilities to authoritatively allocate goals were weakened and, in time, eroded.

Largely due to the incapacity of the imamate to implement political coercion without seemingly violating prescribed traditional laws, internal conflicts developed and led to political change. Political change is the alteration of old values for new ones or, specifically, the alteration of goals and aims. [10] Such change can either reinforce legitimacy or weaken it, strengthen central-

ization of authority or decentralize it, lead to greater harmony
and equality within the system or greater disharmony and inequal-
ity.[11] The system must make a choice; the choice it adopts
determines its ability to endure.

As a sacred-collectivity system, the imamic regime was
religiously oriented. As a collective unit, the regime applied
Zeidi law as the source through which alien ideas and beliefs
could be challenged and destroyed. The imams, as upholders
of Zeidism, as guardians of God's law, and as descendants of
the Prophet Mohammed in temporal and civil matters, were not
averse to calling wars against alien ideas and nonbelievers.
They viewed modernism as a danger to the moral and ethical
fiber of their community. The spiritual purity of their subjects
was to be preserved. Consequently, a contradiction within the
political system developed. On the one hand, the imams pursued
a policy of isolationism aimed at safeguarding the spiritual purity
of their subjects. On the other, they sought modern technology
to conduct their resistance to the incursions of modernism into
Yemen.

Modernism is a complex term for a simple definition. It
has been defined as the development of mass communication,
industrialism, urbanization, and decentralization of authority,
greater individual liberties, and greater social mobility.[12] It
is "a process of increasing complexity in human affairs within
which the polity must act."[13] However, a more meaningful
definition of modernism is given by Charles A. Micaud in his
book, Tunisia: The Politics of Modernization:

> Modernity is an opening up of the creative powers
> of ordinary people; it involves an appreciation of
> their rights and potentialities as individuals, of
> their capacities for expression, for happiness,
> for knowledge.[14]

Micaud recognizes that modernization involves certain economic,
political, and social changes, which he summarized:

> (1) The authority of the ancien régime gives way
> to the rule of the people, and ideally, to the doctrine
> that they are equal before the law to which they
> individually consent. (2) The old social units,
> such as the family, village, or tribe, become sub-
> ordinated to a national community; they are replaced
> as agents of social integration by new voluntary
> organizations, such as trade unions and political

parties. (3) An old elite based on birth either dies out or becomes assimilated into a new elite based on achievement and education. (4) Traditional values are to a large extent undermined by a new faith— essentially the belief in material progress through the efficient use of human beings and technical innovations for maximum production.[15]

Modernism is the transformation in ideas, concepts, and creativity. It promotes change, innovation, and science.

The seeming violations of traditional values by the imams and their coercive political decisions were reinforced by external (regional and international) pressures to modernize the state. This weakened the political entity in Yemen. However, when political and economic changes were adopted, the combined elements of internal conflicts and external penetrations (the source of modernistic ideas) had so far advanced that the system was unable to remain intact. The Revolution of 1962 in Yemen ousted the sacred-collectivity system and replaced it with a relatively secular one.

The transformation of Yemen from an isolationist sacred-collectivity system to a relatively secular-libertarian system whose doors are open to the outside world involved a conflict between traditionalism and modernity. "Traditionalism is a self-conscious and deliberative insistence upon, and more specifically a harkening back to, such values and beliefs, often embodied in and symbolized by habits, customs, and the like."[16] It poses a serious problem to political and economic changes, especially when it embodies religious precepts. In practice, however, traditionalists attempt to preserve those values essential to their personal lives against the onslaught of modernity. The struggle between the Yemeni modernist and the Yemeni traditionalist was by no means local. It was a regional conflict that dated back to the 1950s and continued through the 1960s. Originally a struggle of verbal assaults between traditionalists and modernists, it became an armed conflict that centered in Yemen and threatened to involve the major powers.

The conflict between the Yemeni modernist and the Yemeni traditionalist was a power struggle reinforced by opposing ideas on the state of things. Ideology, as a doctrine to be applied to formulating new ideas and concepts, was lacking in Yemeni modernists. Consequently, modernists were confused. In their search for an ideology, they found Arab nationalism, which became a source of strength. Through Arab nationalism, modernists attacked the imamate regime for its reluctance to change.

Yemeni traditionalists, on the other hand, had an ideology in the Zeidi doctrine, which was reinforced by Islam. They tended to be satisfied with the status quo and favored gradual change so that traditional patterns could adapt. Their conceptual framework was already available in the prescribed Zeidi laws. Thus, they strenuously fought to preserve the traditional system and maintain coherency, continuity, and stability in the polity.

PROPOSITIONS FOR THE EXAMINATION

Since this book is concerned with the internal conflicts and external penetrations that influenced change in Yemen, and since it aims to identify those forces by examining Yemen's internal politics and regional and international associations, several theories are necessary to its inquiry:

- That modernization is tantamount to political, social, and economic changes.
- That nationalism is the strongest modernization instrument and the most dangerous to peace, progress, and stability. It is a generative force that arouses the masses into emotional outbursts leading to change.
- That political stability results from political and social mobility in the system. Without such mobility, the system becomes stagnant and unresponsive to popular demands. Therefore, dissident movements are formed with the ultimate goal of weakening the political authority of those in command of the political and social systems.
- That one cannot separate or isolate the study of Yemen without due regard to its intrinsic and historical place in the Arab world, and, by this virtue, one cannot ignore East-West interests and involvements.
- That culture, history, and ethnic background determine the development of a state in relation to its neighbors.
- That shared values within a polity help to reinforce the continuity of established institutions; the absence of shared values results in a reverse reaction.
- That the allocation of resources or goals that are to be effectively implemented requires a strong adherence by those in possession of authority to established values and beliefs that are cherished in the system; otherwise, resistance is formed and confusion results.
- That the infusion of new ideas and methods into the system helps to preserve traditionally held values and beliefs, to

increase the ruler's ability to allocate goals, and to enhance the ruler's legitimacy. Therefore, continuity and change are made possible.

NOTES

1. Dana Adams Schmidt, Yemen: The Unknown War (New York: Holt, Rinehart, and Winston, 1968).

2. Manfred Halpern, "A Redefinition of the Revolutionary Situation." Journal of International Affairs 23 (1969):54-75.

3. Karl W. Deutsch, Politics and Government: How People Decide Their Fate (New York: Houghton Mifflin, 1970), p. 138.

4. David Apter, The Politics of Modernization (Chicago: University of Chicago Press, 1965), pp. 33-34.

5. Ibid., pp. 28-31.

6. Ibid., p. 32.

7. Ibid., p. 31.

8. Ibid., pp. 31-32.

9. Carl J. Friedrich, Man and His Government: An Empirical Theory of Politics (New York: McGraw-Hill, 1963), p. 232.

10. Robert Stookey, Political Change in Yemen: A Study of Values and Legitimacy (Ph.D. dissertation, University of Texas at Austin, 1972), p. 22.

11. Ibid.

12. Gabriel Almond and James Coleman, eds., The Politics of the Developing Areas (Princeton: Princeton University Press, 1960), p. 532.

13. David Apter, The Politics of Modernization, p. 34.

14. Charles A. Micaud, Tunisia: The Politics of Modernization (London: Praeger, 1964), p. ix.

15. Ibid., p. x.

16. Carl J. Friedrich, Man and His Government, p. 614.

CHRONOLOGY OF EVENTS

628 A.D. — Yemen accepts Islam.

740 — Zeidi sect of Islam is founded by Zeid ibn Ali al-Abidin.

889 — Yahya ibn al-Hussein becomes first imam of Yemen.

1839 — Great Britain occupies the port city of Aden.

1904 — Yahya ibn Hamid al-Din becomes imam.

1918 — Imam Yahya enters Sanaa. Independence from Ottoman rule proclaimed.

1926 — Yemen signs treaty of friendship with Italy.

1928 — Yemen signs a 10-year treaty of commerce and friendship with the Soviet Union.

1934 — Yemen declares war on Saudi Arabia.

May — Treaty of Taif with Saudi Arabia ends conflict.

1935 — "Society of Struggle" is formed.

1944 — "Free Yemeni Movement" is created.

1945 — Arab League is created. Yemen becomes a member.

1947 — Yemen joins the United Nations.

1948 — Imam Yahya is assassinated. Coup d'etat lead by Abdullah al-Wazir is proclaimed. Ahmad Hamid al-Din defeats coup and declares himself imam of Yemen.

1952 — Egyptian Revolution is proclaimed. A republic is formed.

1954 — Nasser comes to power.

1955 — Yemen sends delegation to Bandung Conference on nonaligned nations. Diplomatic relations are established between Yemen and the Soviet Union. Coup d'etat lead by Imam Ahmad's brother, Abdullah, is proclaimed. It is defeated, and al-Badr is proclaimed crown prince.

1956 — Yemen establishes diplomatic relations with the People's Democratic Republic of China. Imam Ahmad goes to Jeddah to sign the Jeddah Military Pact with Egypt and Saudi Arabia. The Suez War takes place.

1958 — Yemen joins the United Arab Republic in Confederation, forming the United Arab States.

1959 — Imam Ahmad goes to Italy for medical treatment. Al-Badr attempts to reform the system.

1961 — United Arab Republic is terminated. Imam Ahmad is wounded in an assassination attempt in Hodeidah. United Arab States is terminated.

1962
> September 18 — Imam Ahmad dies. Crown Prince al-Badr becomes the new imam.
> September 26 — Revolution in Yemen is declared, proclaiming the end of the imamate. Sallal becomes head of the new republic.
> September 27 — Egypt sends expeditionary force into Yemen in support of the new republic.
> Saudi Arabia begins arming royalists.
> December 19 — The United States recognizes the Yemen Arab Republic (Y.A.R.)

1963
> May 4 — The United Nations sends an observation mission of 200 people to Yemen to oversee the disengagement of the conflicting forces.

1964
> September — Alexandria meeting between Nasser and Faisal to negotiate on Yemen takes place.
> November — Faisal becomes king of Saudi Arabia.

1965
> April — Mohammed Zubeiri is assassinated. The Khamir Conference is convened.
> October — The Jeddah Agreement is signed by Egypt and Saudi Arabia.

1966
> November — The Haradh Conference is held between royalists and republicans.

1967
> June — The Arab-Israeli War takes place.
> August — The Khartoum Agreement is formed between Saudi Arabia and Egypt. Both states vow to end the Yemeni conflict.
> December — Egyptian forces in Yemen withdraw.

1968 — The British leave South Yemen. The National Liberation Front seizes power.

1969 — Royalist military resistance stagnates.

1970 — The Reconciliation Agreement between royalists and republicans is established.
> December — Constitution of Y.A.R. goes into effect.

1971
> March — Abdul Rahman al-Iryani becomes president of Y.A.R. under terms of the constitution.
> June — "Open-door policy" is adopted.

1972
> January — Central Planning Organization is established.
> December — First Three-Year Development Program goes into effect.

1974
June — Military comes into power, institutes "Corrective Measures," and suspends the constitution.

1976
Summer — First Five-Year Plan is inaugurated.

1977
October — President al-Hamdi is assassinated and succeeded by Colonel Ahmad al-Ghashmi.

1978
June — President al-Ghashmi is assassinated and succeeded by Colonel Ali Abdullah Saleh. President Salemi Rubay Ali is killed in rivalry with Abdul Fatah Ismail in South Yemen.

1979
February — The People's Democratic Republic of South Yemen (PDRY) attacks Y.A.R.

March — Arab League cease-fire goes into effect. Hostilities between Y.A.R. and PDRY end.

1980 — Census taken by Y.A.R. indicates that population of the country is 8.5 million.

October — Abdul Karim al-Iryani becomes prime minister.

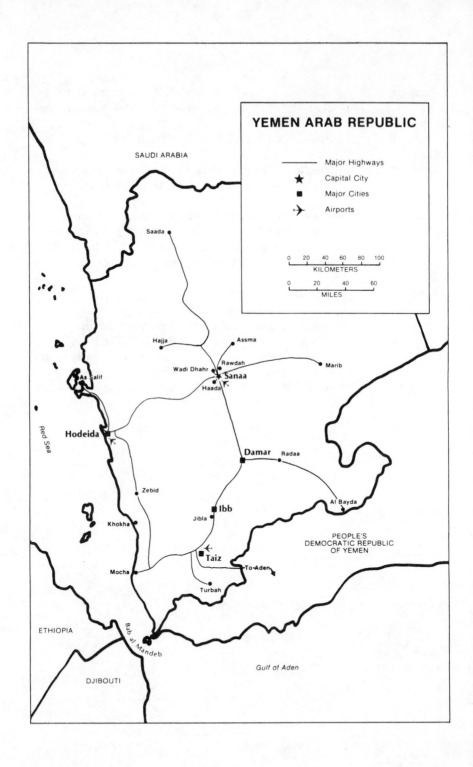

PART I
Era of
Isolationism

1

FACTORS THAT
INFLUENCED ISOLATIONISM

Yemen became independent from Ottoman rule in 1918 after almost five decades of continuous war. An independent imamate regime was created in Yemen. In order to safeguard its newly won independence, the imamate government adopted an isolationist policy. It neither wished to be internationally involved nor regionally entangled in Arab political movements. The immediate need of the regime was the preservation of independence and the perpetuation of the sovereignty of the state.

A strict policy of isolationism marked the entire reign of Imam Yahya ibn Mohammed Hamid al-Din (1904-48). Three factors helped mold the attitude of his regime in its conduct and policy decisions: the geographic location of Yemen, the violations of the Zeidi doctrine of Islam, and the economy.

THE GEOGRAPHIC LOCATION OF YEMEN

The location of Yemen on the map has always interested foreign powers. It is situated to the southwest of Saudi Arabia, bordering the Red Sea along the Strait of Bab al-Mandab. The country has 300 miles of coastline that form its western frontier, stretching from Bab al-Mandab on the southwestern extremity of the Arabian Peninsula to a point south of Najran in Saudi Arabia. Its frontiers from there are irregular, following eastward to Rub al-Khali (the Empty Quarter). In this area, the frontier runs in a general northeasterly direction and fades out in the upper reaches of Wadi Bana. Yemen occupies an area of approximately 75,000 square miles with a population estimated to be 8.5 million.[1]

The population of Yemen is divided almost equally between Shiite Zeidi and Sunnite Shaf'i sects of Islam. Approximately 500,000 from the total population belong to the Sayyid clan,[2] descendants of the Prophet Mohammed from which the imams are derived. The Sayyids are considered to possess baraka (blessing). Consequently, they enjoy a special status in Yemen. The majority of Sayyids belong to the Zeidi sect.

Yemen's geographical contrasts are apparent in three regions: the central highlands, the lowlands and "Tihama" along the Red Sea coast, and the eastern hills that descend into the desert of Rub al-Khali. The mountains in the highlands extend up to 12,000 feet above sea level. All three regions can produce enough agricultural goods to feed the entire population and to supply export demands. Rainfall is sufficient in the highlands, while the Tihama region has underground running streams only 30 feet from the surface.

The highlands of Yemen serve not only as a protective natural barrier to foreign incursions but also as molders of character. The sheer roughness of the rocky mountains and of the terrain gave the tribes of the highlands characteristics unique in that area of the world. The tribes were generally aggressive, individualistic, and austere. Consequently, they were never completely dominated by foreign invaders. However, tribal allegiance prevented the development of a controlling inter-tribal authority and this increased intratribal conflicts. The lack of a central authority in the highlands made life rather dangerous. A segmented authority prevailed throughout most of Yemen's history.

The highland tribes were predominantly Zeidis belonging to the two largest tribal confederations, Bakil and Hashid. These two tribes controlled the highlands, and no one could control Sanaa and Yemen without the support of the two confederations.[3] The confederations not only provided the imams with soldiers to wage wars but also with governors and administrators.

The lowlands, on the other hand, were vulnerable to outside pressure and occupation. The Tihama people were predominantly interested in commerce and business rather than in preserving their freedom. Consequently, they were subjugated on many occasions by outsiders. Their plight was compounded by geography. The lowland people were hedged in since the only area to which they could easily migrate was across the Red Sea. They were not able to develop a strong, viable military force. As a result, they relied upon the highlands for protection.

The eastern hills region is similar to that of the highlands. The people of this area were austere and aggressive. However, because they were less numerous than the highland tribes, they were not able to dominate other tribes or to extend their territory. In this area, segmented authority was apparent, and the imams had difficulties in subjugating the people.

On the north, east, and south, Yemen is almost literally surrounded by desert. It, therefore, had little continuous contact with other active political systems. Geographical isolation prevented political growth and economic progress. The fact that foreign invaders were never able to dominate the highland tribes impeded political growth and increased isolationist tendencies within the highlands. The individualistic and aggressive behavior of the tribes in the highlands also contributed to the lack of political growth and was augmented by the absence of a central controlling authority.

VIOLATIONS OF ZEIDISM

In 628 A.D., Yemen accepted the new religion of Islam. Two centuries later, a religiopolitical group, the Zeidi sect, emerged in Yemen and transformed the country into a society akin to tradition. This sect ruled Yemen for more than 1,000 years.

The Zeidi sect was founded by Zeid abn Ali al-Abidin (740 A.D.). Zeid was the grandson of Ali, the fourth caliph (successor) after the death of the Prophet Mohammed. Ali was the nephew and son-in-law of the Prophet, having married Mohammed's daughter, Fatimah.

The Zeidi sect of Islam is also a sect of Shii, meaning party, which refers specifically to the party of Ali. The Shiis consider Ali the rightful successor to the Prophet Mohammed in temporal and secular matters, denying this to all others. They contend that succession to the caliphate is hereditary.

The Shiis are considered the second major religious sect in Islam. The other is the Sunni sect, which is considered the orthodoxy in Islam since it believes that succession to the caliphate is nonhereditary and since it acknowledges Ali only as the fourth caliph to the Prophet. The Zeidis are in agreement with this contention and readily accept the three caliphs that preceded Ali. However, they assert that only a member of Ahl al-Beit (descendants of the Prophet) can be an imam. An imam is considered the leader of his community in religious and secular affairs. To the Zeidis, the imam is amir al-mu'minin (commander of the faithful).

The Zeidis have been considered mu'tazilites, or rationalists, the "Protestants of Islam."[4] The essence of their beliefs is that reason determines human acts. People are free to perform according to the dictates of reason.

The Zeidi doctrine adheres to the principle of election as the basis of succession. The process involved in electing an imam is democratically sound. An imam is chosen by his peers, Ahl al-Hal wa al-Agd, the ulema (religious leaders), the chiefs of the tribes, and community leaders in conformity with the Shari'a (Islamic law), which specifies the imam's qualifications, rights, and duties. A Zeidi candidate for the imam must meet 14 requirements, which are divided into the physical and mental aspects of the candidate.[5] Among the most important qualifications a candidate must meet: he must be an adult male from Ahl al-Beit, a mujtahid (intellectual), and a military figure of unquestioned courage.[6]

The election of an imam is done at a meeting of the three electing groups (ulema, chiefs of the tribes, and community leaders), who represent the Islamic community as a whole. Once chosen, the imam must abide by the Qur'an, the Shari'a, the Hadith (Sayings of the Prophet), and by consultation with members of the imam's government as well as with the people. The Zeidis adhere closely to the Qur'anic dictate: "Consult them in their welfare." However, the imams in Yemen tended to delegate little or no authority and instead sought power at the expense of other rivals for the office. This prevented the growth of a durable political system and created political conflicts and wars. Hence no imam was able, with the exceptions of Mutawakkil Ismail in the seventeenth century and Yahya ibn Mohammed Hamid al-Din and his son, Ahmad, in the twentieth century, to spread his hegemony over the entire country. The problem was compounded by the individualistic attitude of tribes that did not readily accept the authority of an imam. Tribal allegiance was first and foremost. Tribal loyalty was transferrable from one ruler to another or to whoever ruled the district. This condition persisted throughout the history of Yemen and still persists today. The imams were forced to adopt the medieval practice of holding the eldest sons of tribal leaders as hostages to ensure tribal loyalty and to reduce tribal rebelliousness. This practice was also used to counter tribal assabiyyah (partisanship), which caused intertribal conflicts and vendettas. The hostage system continued well into the twentieth century until it was abolished by Imam Mohammed al-Badr ibn Ahmad Hamid al-Din several days before the demise of the imamate in the Revolution of 1962. Nonetheless, the imams developed a phenomenal aura that, to a degree, controlled tribal conflict and discontent. Imamic charisma was determined by a strong personality and reinforced by the belief held by many Yemenis that the imams, as descendants of the Prophet, had the blessings of God. They were considered more spiritually deserving to be community leaders.

Zeidism purports to be a just ideology since it is based on Islam. The imam, as the highest administrator in religious and civil matters, is required to uphold the welfare of the community. He is to encourage justice and to govern according to the dictates of God's law (Shari'a). The imam must recognize that his powers are derived from God and from the consent of his subjects. As such, he is not absolutely sovereign. Sovereignty in Islam is embodied in the Shari'a, nation, and imam or leader.[7] The latter is the guardian of the Shari'a and the chosen of the people.[8]

The Zeidi doctrine initially developed in Yemen as a direct result of Yahya ibn al-Hussein, the first imam of Yemen. He established precedents in his political conduct and in his religious attitudes that have become a part of the Zeidi law. As the father of the Sayyids in Yemen, he is viewed with reverence.

Yahya ibn al-Hussein entered Yemen in 889 A.D., after a group of Yemenis representing the various highland tribes went to the Hejaz to urge him to come to Yemen to be their imam. After the tribes gave Yahya their allegiance, he went to Yemen.

Although the tribes had sought him to serve as a benevolent, nonpartisan mediator and religious teacher, Yahya began immediately to institute the Islamic Shari'a and to create a systematic administrative machinery for the implementation of Islamic laws. He believed that his duty as imam was to propagate Islam by education and, if necessary, by the use of force. As a member of Ahl al-Beit, Yahya thought himself to be divinely designated and spiritually motivated. His subjects were to be made aware of their responsibilities to God, to the Prophet, and to him as their imam. When, however, the tribes reneged on their declared allegiance to him, Yahya abruptly left Yemen for the Hejaz. During the years 889-93 A.D., the situation in north Yemen deteriorated. Intertribal conflicts again erupted. This was compounded by a two-year period of drought. The tribes interpreted these events as God's punishment for their broken promise to Yahya ibn al-Hussein. Their leaders, once again, went to the Hejaz to prevail upon Yahya to return to Yemen to be their imam. They were anxious to atone for their error.

Yahya returned to Yemen in 893 A.D. The imamate thereafter became an established institution, which lasted until 1962. Yahya's reign lasted 14 years. He took the title of al-Hadi, the guide.

Upon entering Yemen, Yahya declared to his subjects the reciprocal obligations between himself and them. In the proclamation, Imam Yahya said:

> Oh people! I summon you to what Allah had commanded me to summon you to: to Allah's Book, to the traditions of his Prophet, and to obey what is right and forbid what is evil. We must follow what the Book has commanded and reject what it prohibits. In order that we and you can struggle by the right and we and you, together, can prohibit what is evil. [9]

He continued:

> Oh, people! I place on myself four conditions: to govern according to Allah's Book and His Messenger's (blessing and peace be upon him and his descendants) teachings; to favor you before me in things that Allah has decreed between you and me; to uphold your welfare above mine; and to advance before you to meet mine and your enemy. I place two conditions on you: to consult and advise me secretly and openly in accordance to Allah's commands, and to obey me so long as I obey Allah. If I violate my obedience to Allah, I have no right to your obedience; if I alter or distort Allah's Book and His Messenger's teachings, I have no right (to rule) over you. [10]

On another occasion, Imam Yahya ibn al-Hussein was said to have asserted that "between me and you is the Book, word for word. If I violate even a word therein, I deserve not your obedience. Your duty would be to fight me." [11]

Imam Yahya's concern with propagating Islam was evident in most of his proclamations. Adhering to and implementing the faith was his primary duty. Many Yemenis had not experienced the burden of religious laws and were rather rebellious toward his authority. In order to implement the new ideology, the imam had to constantly go to war. By so doing, he was expanding the community of Islam. However, military campaigns required the imam to satisfy the tribes supporting his ventures and his leadership. Such satisfaction was granted either through material inducements or through status promotions. The tribes were not idealistically motivated to spread the faith. This phenomenon continued to plague the imams in the succeeding centuries. No imam was able to defeat rival claimants, heretics, or foreign invaders without material inducements or status promotions of tribal chiefs.

Nowhere was Imam Yahya's endeavor to enforce Islamic laws more apparent than in the collection of the zakat, taxes on livestock and commodities. He preoccupied himself in collecting the zakat in order to discharge Islamic obligations and to prosecute military campaigns against heretics from the revenues obtained. Imam Yahya, however, was scrupulous in using the zakat only to benefit Islam and his people. He sent agents to the countryside to collect the zakat with a warning that due diligence and just assessments be applied. He commanded his agents that if a citizen owned part of a plot, that citizen's share of the harvest was to be proportioned before assessment. Imam Yahya was adhering closely to the Zeidi dictate that the zakat should not be misused or misdirected. Misuse of the zakat is a violation of Islamic law and, hence, reprehensible.

Imam Yahya ibn al-Hussein was concerned with the moral image of his administration. He desired to see his regime accepted by the people because of its adherence to Islamic laws. Thus, the imam directed an agent of his, appointed to govern the outlying districts around Saada in northern Yemen, to proceed to that area in peace and dignity. He was to invoke the name of Allah, to rent for himself a modest accommodation, to demand nothing for his personal use, to place those gifts given to him by the people to beit al-mal (public treasury), to command what was right and forbid what was evil in accordance with Allah's book, to teach the people to pray, to struggle in the right, and to collect the zakat. He should make sure that taxes on crops grown on land watered by rain or flowing streams be levied 10 percent and that those crops grown on land watered from wells or manmade canals be levied 5 percent.[12] Imam Yahya then urged his agent to remember that Allah knows every act of every actor and rewards them accordingly.[13]

Imam Yahya ibn al-Hussein endeavored to create a political system spiritually oriented and hierarchical in its form. The segmented patterns that were there before his arrival had to be subordinated or destroyed so that the new system could be realized. However, the new values that Imam Yahya introduced to Yemen could not be completely accepted by the tribes since they impinged on tribal values. He was accepted by them as their religious and civil leader, but when his rules threatened tribal identities, the tribes revolted. This phenomenon troubled all the succeeding imams, and they were hard pressed to control tribal rebelliousness.

The greatest contribution Imam Yahya ibn al-Hussein was able to make was the creation of a central, dominating figure who acted as the final arbiter in intertribal conflicts and disputes. The implementation of Islamic laws introduced into Yemen a semblance of order and justice, hitherto missing in Yemen's segmented society. Imam Yahya was able to maintain the spiritual orientation of the office of the imam by guarding the principles on which his authority to rule were based.

However, some of the ulemas and imams that followed him tended to explain Zeidism in accordance to their own interpretations, which were affected to some degree by their ambitions and political interests. Consequently, Zeidism suffered, becoming a relatively stagnant political ideology rather than the enlightened and progressive political and religious movement it was meant to be (see Chapters 2 and 3).

THE ECONOMY

The Yemeni economy is predominantly agricultural. From approximately 80 to 85 percent of the people derive their livelihood from the land. The land in Yemen is, however, fertile, and crops of all varieties grow abundantly. The most common agricultural products found in Yemen are wheat, coffee, barley, corn, and durra (a kind of grain sorghum). Fruits are also in abundance. There had been speculation that Yemen possessed mineral resources of sufficient quantities that, if exploited, could have made Yemen an economic giant in the Arabian Peninsula. Nevertheless, Yemen remained economically stagnant during the reign of Imam Yahya ibn Mohammed Hamid al-Din (1904-48). Two factors account for Yemen's lack of economic progress: Imam Yahya's adamant refusal to open Yemen to foreign economic interests and the lack of such modern communication facilities as radios, telephones, roads, and so on.

Before Yemen became independent in 1918, foreign interest in Yemen had been apparent. The French and the Italians wanted to establish favorable economic positions in Yemen. After independence, the pace of foreign interest in Yemen increased. The French, the Italians, and the Russians showed a keen interest in creating an advantageous economic status in the country.

The French and Italian attempts to establish an economic foothold in Yemen were meant to supplement their efforts on the opposite shores of the Red Sea. The efforts of both France and Italy failed because Imam Yahya viewed outside interests

in Yemen as potentially dangerous to the independence of his
country. He feared that foreign ideas in Yemen could conceivably
corrupt the spiritual purity of his subjects and undermine his
political leadership. The imam was also fearful of becoming
involved in big-power rivalry in the area. Consequently, he
rejected French efforts to search for mineral resources and
refused to conclude a treaty of friendship with the French until
they recognized his sovereignty over Aden and the protectorate,
which was under British control.[14] The imam also refused to
accept Italian interest in his country. Although he concluded
a treaty of friendship with Italy, Italian investments in Yemen
were not permitted to mature.

Soviet interest in Yemen was motivated by a desire to establish access to warm-water ports in the Mediterranean area.
Yemen was viewed by the Soviet authorities as a stepping stone
in gaining control over the Red Sea area. By so doing, they
could have controlled the Red Sea routes to and from the Mediterranean area. This would have undermined British interests
not only in Egypt but also in India.

The Soviet Union was anxious to break its geographic isolation and sought to create some form of political, economic, and
diplomatic relationship with the Middle Eastern countries. Yemen
seemed likely to accept Russian overtures to counter British
presence in Aden and the protectorate.

Soviet efforts to create an atmosphere of cooperation with
the Yemeni regime bore fruitful results in 1928 with the signing
of a 10-year treaty of commerce and friendship. Under its
provisions, Yemen was recognized as an independent kingdom.
The treaty was extended for another 10 years in 1938. During
these years, the Soviet Union tried to cultivate its friendship
with Yemen in order to offset Italian influence on the eastern
shores of the Red Sea.[15] It also sought to counterbalance
Western political and economic interests in the peninsula. The
Soviet Union unloaded petroleum products and exhibited agricultural machinery in Hodeida and Sanaa. Imam Yahya's apprehensions obstructed Soviet attempts to make inroads into Yemen.
Like France and Italy, the Soviet Union failed to establish a
favorable economic position in Yemen.

The deterioration of the Yemeni economy was also partially
caused by almost five decades of war with Turkey and by fre-
quent droughts. Yemen also possessed few, if any, improved
roads. Trucks and other transport vehicles, which were few
in number, were compelled to use mountain trails that were
hazardous. The conditions of the transport vehicles declined
rapidly since only cosmetic repairs could be made on them.

Consequently, truckers charged exorbitant rates for transporting goods and commodities from one area of the state to another.

The economic plight of Yemen was further aggravated by the conversion of coffee plantations to qat areas. Qat is a mild narcotic green leaf that grows easily and with little attention and care. Since many Yemenis chew qat (approximately 60 to 75 percent),[16] the product has a profitable market. Coffee, which was the principle export commodity (in a normal year, about 80,000 bales or more than 12.5 million pounds of Yemeni coffee used to be exported),[17] was drastically curtailed as an exportable item because Yemen received a substantial revenue from the export of qat to Aden and the protectorate and to areas on the opposite shore of the Red Sea.[18]

The lack of modern transportation and communication facilities also helped to stagnate the Yemeni economy. Agricultural methods remained unchanged through the centuries. Imam Yahya refused to import modern agricultural machinery for use in Yemen.[19] Moreover, indigenous small industry (soap, saddle harnesses, shoes, arms, glass, and jewelry) declined as a result of the regime's indifference to economic development. Only after the 1948 coup d'etat and, more specifically, after the Suez War of 1956, were attempts undertaken by the central government to rejuvenate the Yemeni economy. Foreign investments were encouraged in Yemen. Nonetheless, Yemen suffered economic neglect during the entire reign of Imam Yahya ibn Mohammed.

Imam Yahya's adamant refusal to accept foreign economic investments in Yemen must be viewed in the context of his immediate objective, that is, to maintain security and independence. The imam could not be impervious to imperialism or to the competition for outside possessions by the great powers of Europe. Yemen itself had been geographically partitioned into two entities by Great Britain in 1839. At the time Britain took over Aden, Yemen was under Turkish rule. The imamate regime located in north-central Yemen was fighting the Turkish presence. It was unable to mount any resistance to British incursions. Moreover, Aden and its adjacent areas had no central authority. The different principalities of the area were ruled by sheiks and sultans, and all tended to function autonomously. British access into the area was, therefore, relatively easy.

The British occupation of Aden was construed by the Yemenis as the gravest outside invasion to have occurred because it preserved British presence in the area for a long time. It also gave rise to an independent state in 1968 (the People's Republic of South Yemen), thus dividing Yemen into two parts.

Britain was able to stretch its political influence to the entire Arabian Peninsula from Aden to Jordan and Iraq in the upper north.[20] British presence in the Arabian Peninsula was also detrimental to the fledgling Arab nationalism that had begun to stir during World War I.

British intentions in the Arab world became evident to the Yemeni government immediately after World War I. Yemen witnessed the complete partitioning of Arab lands by both Britain and France and the abrogation of promises made to the Arabs by Great Britain to induce the Arabs to rise in revolt against Ottoman rule.

Against such a background, Imam Yahya showed his political acumen by remaining aloof to international involvements after independence was achieved in Yemen. He accepted only minimal foreign economic assistance. By steering his nation onto an isolationist path, the imam was guaranteeing its independence. He was not even willing to become involved in regional Arab politics, even though he was considered to be the most likely individual to take a leadership role in the Arab world.[21] Such a belief in the imam was enhanced by the popular attitude that he was one of the "most knowledgeable Arab kings in the 1920's in religion, jurisprudence, and language."[22]

NOTES

1. Yemen Arab Republic (Arab Information Center, June 1973), p. 2.

2. William Brown reports in his article, "The Yemeni Dilemma," that the Sayyids in Yemen numbered 300,000 in 1963. Middle East Journal 17 (Autumn 1963):350. Ibrahim al-Kibsi, deputy foreign ministry, asserts that Brown's figure falls short of the commonly accepted figure of 500,000. Personal interview, September 24, 1975.

3. Harold Ingrams, The Yemen: Imams, Rulers, and Revolutions (London: 1933), p. 12.

4. William Spencer, Political Evolution in the Middle East (Philadelphia: J. B. Lippincott, 1962), pp. 321-23.

5. Abdullah ibn Muftah, Sharh al-Azhar ("The Elucidation of the Flowers"), vol. 4 (Cairo: Matba'at al-Ma'bad, 1921), pp. 518-97.

6. Ibid., pp. 518-24.

7. Abd al-Rahman Azzam, The Eternal Message of Mohammed, translated from Arabic by Caesar E. Farha (New York: Devin-Adair, 1964), p. 120.

8. Ibid.

9. Ali ibn Mohammed Abeed Allah al-Abbassi, Sirah al-Hadi ila al-Hag: Yahya ibn al-Hussein ("The Biography of the Guide to the Right: Yahya ibn al-Hussein"), edited by Dr. Sahil Zakkar (Damascus: Daar al-Fikr, 1972), p. 48.

10. Ibid., pp. 48-49.

11. Ibid., p. 51.

12. Ibid., pp. 44-46.

13. Ibid., p. 46.

14. Eric Macro, Yemen and the Western World since 1571 (London: C. Hurst, 1968), pp. 67-70.

15. Ibid., p. 113.

16. Richard Sanger, The Arabian Peninsula (New York: Cornell University Press, 1954), pp. 262-63.

17. A. Faroughy, Introducing Yemen (New York: Orientalia, 1947), p. 15.

18. Ibid., p. 17.

19. Edgar O'Ballance, The War in the Yemen (Hamden, Conn.: Archon, 1971), p. 35.

20. Zaid Ali al-Wazir, Muhawalat li Fahm al-Mashkelah al-Yamaniah ("Attempts to Understand the Problem of Yemen") (Beirute: al-Sharekah al-Muttahedal lil-Towze', 1968), p. 181.

21. Ibid., p. 52.

22. Amin al-Raihani, Muluk al-Arab ("The Arab Kings"), vol. I (Beirute: Daar al-Raihani lil-Tiba'ah wa al-Nashr, 1960), p. 178.

2

THE WEAKENING OF
TRADITIONALISM

Imam Yahya ibn Mohammed Hamid al-Din was elected imam in conformity with the Zeidi doctrine. He was an energetic, intelligent, and highly motivated man. Through his leadership, Yemen became independent from Turkish rule in 1918.

Imam Yahya inherited a system that had existed for centuries—a system of theocracy, in essence a patriarchal system, wherein the patriarch was given almost total power. His only limitations were the Shari'a and certain traditionally held precepts. Imam Yahya exercised his rule directly; therefore, all government administrative agencies were not independent to perform their functions. They served the will and the bidding of the imam.

Imam Yahya was motivated to transform some age-old values in favor of new ones to consolidate his position. But these endeavors weakened his regime since his attempts infringed on traditionally established patterns of values. The imam was concerned with two principle factors: the role of education and the political aggrandizement of the ruling family.

THE ROLE OF EDUCATION

As the Zeidi imam, Imam Yahya ibn Mohammed felt a deep responsibility for the salvation of his subjects' souls. He felt responsible to God for maintaining the religious purity of his subjects and endeavored to minimize foreign influence in Yemen. Such an attempt meant keeping Yemen isolated from the outside world and keeping a careful scrutiny on all foreigners in Yemen.

Amin al-Rayhani reported that he was kept a virtual prisoner
by Imam Yahya in Sanaa until his credentials from King Hussein
of the Hejaz had been clarified.[1] Other foreigners, Arabs and
non-Arabs, were also watched carefully, and their movements
in the country were restricted. Many foreigners were discour-
aged from entering Yemen, and Yemenis were not permitted to
leave Yemen without the imam's direct approval. Such a policy
was clearly detrimental to the Yemeni educational system, which
needed improvements.

The regime of Imam Yahya ibn Mohammed placed much
weight on religious schooling and de-emphasized secular education. Imam Yahya went so far as to close a school for girls that
the Turks had opened before they departed.[2]

Until the 1940s, education in Yemen was restricted mostly
to reading, writing, Islamic laws, and Arabic literature. Little
was done to advance science and the arts. Although 500 schools
were opened in the country by 1941 and compulsory education
from the ages of seven to seventeen had been instituted,[3] in
general the schools offered only minimal education, and attendance
was limited. The quality of education could not be compared
with the educational systems outside of Yemen. Many Yemenis
who went abroad in the 1940s and 1950s, supposedly well-educated
by Yemeni standards, had to enroll in foreign high schools to
supplement their educations. A Yemeni scholar declared that
Yemenis sent to Egypt for higher education in the 1950s were so
far behind they had to have special tutors.[4] The same author
declared that only four secondary schools were to be found in
Sanaa, Hodeida, and Taiz. All had no primary curriculum.[5]
There were only two secondary and five elementary schools in
Sanaa in the 1940s. A "scientific" school in Sanaa was founded
in 1925, with an enrollment of 1,000 students.[6] Students were
required to concentrate on Islamic jurisprudence, Arabic literature, and poetry. Enrollment in the Yemeni schools in the 1940s
was reported at 50,000 students.[7]

Education in Yemen was more accessible to urban dwellers
than to rural people because most of the schools were in the
cities. Moreover, only the children of well-to-do families were
able to improve their education since their families were able
to hire tutors. Consequently, only a few Yemenis became well-
educated.

The de-emphasis on secular education was incompatible
with Islamic teachings and Zeidi law. The Prophet Mohammed
encouraged his people to seek knowledge "even in China."
Furthermore, the Arab empire found its glorious achievement
in the arts and sciences. Its contribution to scientific and

artistic development was immense. Imam Yahya's endeavor to limit education constituted a violation of Islamic and traditional values. However, the emphasis placed on Islamic education was an attempt by the imam to lessen spiritually subversive influences from abroad. The imam feared foreign ideas and hoped that by keeping Yemen isolated the spiritual purity of his people would be preserved.

Imam Yahya's educational program, although limited in scope, was rather astounding. The fact that Yemen had 500 schools with an enrollment of 50,000 students by the 1940s spoke well for the imam's educational system. This was made possible even though Yemen's annual national income never exceeded $10 million during the 1920s and 1930s.[8] Comparatively speaking, Yemen was far ahead of Saudi Arabia in the field of education during both decades. Only when oil was found in Saudi soil was Saudi educational progress able to surpass that of Yemen. More specifically, Yemen was still far ahead of Saudi Arabia in education in the early 1950s.

In 1953, Saudi schools, both primary and secondary, numbered 326 with an enrollment of 43,734 students.[9] These figures are far below those attributed to Yemen's educational progress in 1941. Moreover, Saudi income was far greater than that of Yemen in the 1940s and 1950s. In 1953, Saudi income in oil alone was reported to be $200 million.[10] Thus, with the limited resources at Yemen's disposal, education was far more available in Yemen than it was in Saudi Arabia.

THE PRIMACY OF THE HAMID AL-DIN FAMILY

Imam Yahya ibn Mohammed was preoccupied with consolidating his political power in Yemen. In his endeavor to accomplish his task, he emphasized the primacy of his family and altered age-old traditional values, thus creating discordance and opposition.

To consolidate his political power in Yemen, Imam Yahya attempted to reduce tribal unrest, to go to war with Saudi Arabia, and to conclude a treaty of friendship with Great Britain. These tasks were undertaken in the first 16 years of independence.

Reducing Tribal Unrest

The first act taken by Imam Yahya in reducing tribal unrest was in 1928 when he dispatched his son, Prince Ahmad, to

curtail the Zaraniq tribe, located north of Hodeida, from their
rebelliousness. The tribe was effectively stripped of its leaders
and remained docile for a long time. Imam Yahya recognized
that tribal unrest must be checked if security and independence
were to be maintained. He was aware of tribal love for freedom,
and he sought to curb tribal insurrection. Tribal arrogance
and love of freedom was expressed by a Yemeni to Amin al-
Rayhani in 1922. He stated:

> Our country has a good climate and good water.
> But the people are always at war . . . We fought
> the Turks, we fought the tribes, we fought the
> al-Idrisi, and always we fight amongst ourselves
> . . . (the Imam) controls only a small part of Yemen.
> We Yemenis never submit to anyone permanently.
> We love freedom and we fight for it. We will slay
> the closest to us to remain independent. We say
> to the Imam: We don't want this man as our ruler,
> and we appoint our own shiekh, and we tell him:
> You are our ruler; you are our leader . . . And
> if the Imam's appointee refuses (to step down)?
> We slay him.[11]

Tribal unrest in the Tihama region forced the imam to
undertake military campaigns against the tribes in order to
force obedience. The fact that the majority of the people were
Shaf'is who did not accept the virtual leadership of the imam
made the Tihama area susceptible to tribal insurrection. Moreover, the area was a confused region after independence was
achieved. There were three prospective rulers for the region:
Imam Yahya; Mohammed ibn Ali al-Idrisi, ruler of the Province
of Asir located northwest of Yemen; and Great Britain, stationed
in Aden and the protectorate.

Imam Yahya claimed sovereignty over Greater Yemen, which
included the Province of Asir and Aden and the protectorate.
The al-Idrisi contended the imam's claim and held onto the port
city of Hodeida, which the British had bombarded in 1919 and
occupied for a brief period. In the same year, the British
handed the city to al-Idrisi in retaliation for the imam's occupation of certain areas north of Aden that they considered to be
under their jurisdiction.[12]

The people of the Tihama did not wish to be ruled by the
imam, the al-Idrisi, or the British. They believed that the imam
would restrict their commercial business and that the al-Idrisi
would undermine the port city of Hodeida in favor of the port

city of Jaizan in the Province of Asir.[13] But once the city of Hodeida was in the hands of the al-Idrisi, the Tihama people acquiesced to his rule.

Mohammed al-Idrisi died in 1922. He was succeeded by his son, Ali. Ali ibn Mohammed lacked the political acumen of his father. Consequently, he misruled the Tihama region. Tribal disaffection and insurrection became manifest. Many of the tribes requested Imam Yahya to assist them against the misrule of Ali al-Idrisi.[14] Motivated by the disorders in the Tihama, Imam Yahya moved against Ali al-Idrisi. In 1925, the port city of Hodeida was seized by the imam's forces. However, some tribes refused to accept the rule of the imam, notably the Zaraniq and the Quhra tribes, located between the towns of Zebid and Beit al-Faqih. The imam dispatched his son, Prince Ahmad, to dissuade the tribes from political unrest.

Tribal unrest in the eastern hills was not as apparent as tribal unrest in the Tihama region. Nonetheless, it occupied a great part of the imam's attention. The imam was reported to have been away from the capital on several occasions attending to the tribes in the eastern hills. He also used the services of Abdullah al-Wazir, a prominent Sayyid and governor of Damar, in bringing order and security to the eastern hills.

The eastern hills people, although predominantly Zeidis, were averse to accepting a central authority. Their tribal identity was deeply rooted. National sentiment was rather remote. The imam's attempt to enforce the Shari'a and Islamic duties was met with resistance. But the imam persisted, and order and obedience were restored.

Conflict with Saudi Arabia

In 1925, the same year that Ali al-Idrisi was defeated by Imam Yahya, Abdul Aziz al-Saud was crowned king of the Hejaz and sultan of Nejd and dependencies. The Hashemite rule in the Hejaz was ended.

King Abdul Aziz laid claim to the Province of Asir and moved quickly to incorporate it. Imam Yahya viewed the Saudi monarch's move as antagonistic and tried to convince the Saudi king to return the province. Abdul Aziz, however, considered the Province of Asir as being under his protection, and he refused to relinquish it to the imam. In refusing to yield the province to Imam Yahya, Saudi-Yemeni relations were strained.

The relationship between Yemen and Saudi Arabia was further strained because Saudi and Yemeni farmers, close to the borders, tended to graze and water their flocks on each others' territories. Each state accused the other of violating territorial rights. The problem escalated, and in 1934 war erupted between the two Arab states. The war ended on May 20, 1934, with the Treaty of Taif. The conciliation they reached ended hostilities. Yemen ceded the towns of Najran and Jaizan to Saudi Arabia and abandoned its claim to the Province of Asir. Saudi Arabia returned the port city of Hodeida to the imam. The willingness of both to settle for a minor frontier adjustment helped to ease their relationship.

The outcome of the Saudi-Yemeni War was a bitter disappointment to the Yemenis, who believed they should have won the war. It was apparent that the Yemeni army was about to encircle the Saudi forces under Prince Faisal ibn Abdul Aziz, who had taken Hodeida, when the imam ordered a halt to the fighting. No reason was given by the imam for his arbitrary halt to hostilities. There was speculation that the imam did not wish to see two Arab states at war. Nonetheless, the result was traumatic to the Yemenis. For the first time since the imam had become the ruler of Yemen, his decision was questioned. Many Yemenis, Zeidis and Shaf'is, believed that the imam had violated the principle of consultation. They contended that the order to cease fighting was a crucial decision requiring the advice and consent of the imam's government. Moreover, many believed that, had the imam permitted Prince Ahmad to carry on the war, the Yemeni forces would have been successful.[15] An opponent of the imamate described the imam as "rather strange from Imam Yahya of yesterday. He appears paralyzed and empty like a child who surrenders without any reason to surrender."[16]

The settlement between Imam Yahya and King Abdul Aziz eased tensions between the two states. It assured the imam that his northern borders would be respected and that disorder would be ended.

Treaty of Sanaa with Great Britain

The problem with Great Britain was complex and emotional. Imam Yahya had an adverse feeling about the British presence in Aden and the protectorate. As a Zeidi imam, Yahya viewed the British as a danger to his authority in Yemen. The imamate had been stripped of its sovereignty in Aden and the protectorate by the British in 1839. To the imam, Great Britain represented an odious influence to his people, which he feared was spiritually

subversive to Zeidism.[17] In order to remove the British from
occupied Yemeni territory, the imam felt obligated to be receptive
to Italian interests in Yemen and to purchase modern arms for
his army.

Aware of Italian political differences with Great Britain,
Imam Yahya believed that he could use the Italians to counter
British presence in the Arabian Peninsula. A treaty of friendship and amity with Italy was signed in 1926.[18] Italy's positive
response to the imam's move was motivated by its desire to
create a sphere of influence in Yemen and, by so doing, to
establish a link between Africa and the Arabian Peninsula.
Moreover, it was politically and economically possible that Italy
could supplant Great Britain as the major foreign power in the
area.

Italian initiatives in Yemen aroused British fears. The
British could not ignore the Italian-Yemeni treaty since Britain
considered it a danger to British interest in Aden and the protectorate. Moreover, the British were unwilling to permit the
potential threat of Italian control of the Strait of Bab al-Mandab,
since the Italians already occupied Eritrea. As the only channel
of the Red Sea into the Gulf of Aden, the strait offered complete
control of Suez shipping and communication. The British were
also unwilling to place their commercial interests at the mercy
of a potential adversary. It was imperative to them that Italian
interest in Yemen be frustrated. British fears were also compounded by the imam's friendly overtures to the Soviet Union.
The Soviet-Yemeni Treaty of Friendship in 1928 seemed to have
given credence to the speculation that the imam was toying
"with the idea of playing off the democracies against the dictator-
ships."[19]

British fears of Imam Yahya's diplomatic initiatives were
premature because the imam could not accept the possibility of
Italian presence in Yemen without jeopardizing Yemen's sovereignty. But the imam's actions permitted him to receive Italian
arms in return for preferential trade relations and the employ-
ment of Italian doctors and technicians.[20]

Imam Yahya's agreements with both Italy and the Soviet
Union were achieved without establishing diplomatic relations
with either state. The imam's success in gaining the support
of foreign states without jeopardizing Yemen's isolationism and
sovereignty won him the praise of his people and helped to
strengthen his position at home.[21]

In an attempt to modernize his army, Imam Yahya purchased
modern military equipment from other states, specifically, from
Italy. But Yemen lacked an army of trained personnel. Thus

in 1936, the imam sent a group of selected Yemeni cadets to the
Baghdad Military Academy for training and study.

Soon after the arrival of the Yemeni cadets in Iraq, a
military coup occurred in the host country. Political power
shifted into the hands of the military. The Yemeni cadets witnessed the event firsthand. It can only be surmised that the
Iraqi coup must have had an impact on the political thinking
of the young Yemeni cadets.

Imam Yahya's reaction to the Iraqi coup was to recall the
mission prior to its completion. He arranged for an Iraqi mission
to come to Yemen and instruct his army. The mission was soon
withdrawn when the Iraqi officers spread ideas among the Yemeni
cadets that were construed as contrary to traditional values.

Imam Yahya's problem in dealing with the British in Aden
and the protectorate involved a contradiction of values. He
felt compelled to maintain the traditional Yemeni system, but
circumstances forced him to undertake foreign involvements,
thereby introducing into Yemen modern ideas. Despite the
imam's careful attempts to keep Yemen aloof from international
involvements, such involvements could not be completely avoided.

Once it became apparent to the British that Imam Yahya
was not interested in developing his relationship with Italy and
the Soviet Union, diplomatic efforts between them and the imam
were intensified. The core of the problem involved frontiers.
The imam had refused to accept the frontier line drawn between
Britain and Turkey in 1914, not only because he was not involved
in the negotiations, but also because the lines were not favorable
to Yemen. It became apparent that a new frontier line must be
agreed upon. Thus, on February 11, 1934, the Treaty of Sanaa
was signed, whereby the British recognized the imam as the
king of Yemen and agreed to change the frontier line to one
slightly more favorable to him. However, ambiguities developed
in the Arab-English translation over the term hudud (frontier).[22]
The Arabic text did not contain the word hudud, but rather
the word al-adraf, which had its root meaning in the word darafa
(edge, border). Consequently, Yemen did not agree to the
frontier line as permanent,[23] maintaining that the frontier line
was on the area between the two opposing forces rather than
accepting the actual frontier line separating the domains of the
two countries. Moreover, Yemen contended that its interpretation was correct because the treaty specified that if "doubt
arises as to the interpretation of any of these articles, both
high contracting parties shall rely on the Arabic text."[24] The
treaty, however, suspended the disagreement for 42 years. It
also provided for British nonintervention in Yemen's internal
affairs and for maintenance of the status quo.[25]

The Political Aggrandizement of the
Hamid al-Din Family

Imam Yahya adopted another policy aimed at consolidating
his power by placing members of his family, specifically his
sons, into positions of political and economic authority while
neglecting others more qualified and with better experience.
This alienated many Yemenis.

After independence was achieved, Imam Yahya relegated
many who had fought by his side into either political limbo or
secondary positions in the government. He never explained his
actions. However, it can be surmised that his policy was motivated by the need to ensure his primacy in the system. Many
of his war companions had known the imam informally and were
not awed by his presence. They had achieved their leadership
positions in Yemen largely because of their participation in the
war of independence. Their contribution to Yemen had been
valuable. Their debt to the imam was minimal, hence they could
be critical of the imam on matters of national interest. Moreover,
many believed themselves to be equal to the imam in matters of
Islamic law and jurisprudence. Consequently, their performance
and loyalty to the imam depended on the imam's ability to uphold
traditional values and beliefs. By removing them from their
positions of authority, the imam was promoting his primacy.
Their replacements would be indebted to the imam, awed by his
presence, and unquestionably loyal to his will. His decisions
would be implemented by them without question. The more
powerful and influential positions in the government were assigned
to his sons.

While the imam was able to strengthen his position at the
expense of others, he inadvertently helped to create a source
of discontent. His war companions felt dejected, and their
feelings were transmitted to their sons, many of whom began
to openly conspire against the imam.

Imam Yahya's policy of placing his sons in positions of
political and economic authority was a danger to the imamate.
His attempts to aggrandize his family were construed by many
as dangerous to the continued stability of the polity.

Imam Yahya removed Abdullah al-Wazir and Ali al-Wazir,
two prominent Yemenis, from their positions as governors of
Damar and Taiz respectively, [26] Ali al-Wazir being replaced by
Prince Ahmad. Prince Ahmad had been governor of Hajja, and
his appointment was accepted in light of his experience.

Some criticized Imam Yahya for returning Prince Abdullah
to Hodeida after Abdullah al-Wazir had been temporarily installed

during the prince's absence.[27] The critics felt that Prince
Abdullah was young and immature, and they accused him of
fleeing the city at night, leaving it unprotected during the war
with Saudi Arabia. Eventually, Hodeida fell to Prince Faisal.

Based on these beliefs, his critics considered Prince Abdullah unfit to take the place of Abdullah al-Wazir, who had been
instrumental in pacifying the eastern hills tribes.

The removal of the al-Wazirs from their positions as governors had a negative impact on the relationship between the al-
Wazir and the Hamid al-Din families. Furthermore, tribes loyal
to the al-Wazirs became resentful over their removal.

The removal of the al-Wazirs from their governorships
was followed by a total reorganization of the administration of
the country. Prior to 1944, Yemen had been divided into six
provinces (liwa) whose governors (amir liwa) were appointed
by the imam. The provinces were divided to ensure equal
representation in the administration of the country. The reorganization of the provinces reduced their number to four—
all under the royal family. The central province (capital Damar)
and the northern province (capital Saada) were abolished.[28]
The governorships of Taiz and Hodeida were assigned to Prince
Ahmad and Prince Abdullah. Prince al-Hassan was made governor
of Ibb, and the imam retained the governorship of Sanaa. This
reorganization clearly placed the reins of local government in
the hands of the royal family.

The replacement of the al-Wazirs by the imam, although
reprehensible in the long run, need to be observed in terms of
consensus consideration rather than qualitative deliberation.
The imam was aware that the al-Wazirs had been a distinguished
Yemeni family whose members had contributed scholastically
and intellectually to Yemeni society. Moreover, Ali al-Wazir's
grandfather was the imam of Yemen prior to Mohammed al-
Mansour, Imam Yahya's father. The al-Wazirs' political and
economic influence could not be rivaled by any other family in
Yemen with the exception of the royal family. In order for the
imam to replace the al-Wazirs, he had to consider whether their
replacement would be acceptable to the people. The merits of
the individuals being considered as replacements became secondary. It behooved the imam to appoint his sons to replace the
al-Wazirs, regardless of their ability, in order to satisfy consensus.

POLITICAL DISSENT SETS IN

Political dissent in Yemen probably began immediately after the Saudi-Yemeni War in 1934. It was no longer expressed inarticulately with no concise formulation of how things ought to be. Political dissent after 1934 became organized and articulate. It was expressed by an organization that came to be known as the "Society of Struggle,"[29] under the able leadership of Ahmad al-Muta'a, a Zeidi intellectual considered by many Yemenis as the "father of the Yemeni revolution."[30] Al-Muta'a probed into the misuse of imamate power, and his thinking found a receptive audience with other Yemeni intellectuals who had doubts about the imam's policies and actions.

Between 1935 and 1944, the Society of Struggle fragmented the imam's unified government. By systematically playing on the prejudices of the ministers of the government and on the imam's sons, the society was able to incite friction between them.[31] It was almost able to create factionalism within the regime. The society was successful in making some ministers believe that their work in the services of the imam had been unappreciated. At the same time, the society urged the imam's sons to take active roles in the functions of the government since it was their privilege to do so. Naturally, the interference of the inexperienced princes in the business of the government alienated some members of the imam's regime. The foreign minister, Mohammed Ragheb, resigned as a result of the interference of Prince Hussein in the negotiations with a U.S. mission sent to Yemen to discuss a treaty of friendship with the imam's government. Prince Hussein's conservative political thinking and suspicious mind soon drove the negotiations to a dead end.[32] Only after Ragheb received assurance from the imam that further interference would not occur did he resume negotiations with the U.S. mission. As a result, the U.S. government recognized the imam as king of Yemen.

The Society of Struggle was the only organized movement in Yemen opposing the regime of Imam Yahya. But in 1944, a new movement came into existence to work alongside the society. The movement was founded in Aden by Mohammed Zubeiri and Ahmad Numan, and it was officially called the "Free Yemeni Movement."[33]

The movement advocated liberal reforms and issued a paper called Sawt al-Yaman (the Voice of Yemen). It was successful in contacting Yemenis outside the kingdom and in enlisting their financial and political support. In its early days, it received its greatest success when Prince Ibrahim ibn Yahya fled Yemen and joined the Free Yemenis.

Like the Society of Struggle, the Free Yemeni Movement sought to bring an end to the rule of the Hamid al-Din family.[34] It also sought to create a new imamate, constitutionally based and limited.

The Society of Struggle and the Free Yemeni Movement opposed the refusal of the Yemeni regime to permit political and economic reforms. As liberal thinkers, members could not tolerate what they construed as political oppression practiced by the royal family. Moreover, they opposed Prince Ahmad's succession to the imamate. They refused to see him in early 1945 when he was in Aden. Opposition to Prince Ahmad stemmed from their fear of him. He was known to be highly intelligent with a keen political mind. The Free Yemeni Movement and the Society of Struggle feared that he would in time succeed his father. It became imperative to frustrate his claim.

Prince Ahmad, as early as 1927, had been considered heir apparent by many Yemenis. Although Imam Yahya did not pressure the ulema to give their allegiance to Ahmad, he did not hinder Ahmad's claim. The imam was endeavoring to ensure an orderly transition by tacitly accepting Prince Ahmad as his heir apparent. However, his attempt was incompatible with Zeidi practices, and it undermined the aspirations of several aristocratic families who had previously produced imams. Moreover, it deprived the ulema of their function to choose the next imam unburdened by the imam's personal objectives. It also "intensified the hostility between Ahmad and several of his numerous brothers, some of whom were also plausible contenders and had popular sympathy."[35]

Fearing the continuity of the Hamid al-Din rule, members of the Society of Struggle, in collusion with the Free Yemenis, began to conspire for the eviction of the royal family from power. Recognizing the religiopolitical society of Yemen as a community yet unwilling to accept the dissolution of the imamate, the leaders of the Society of Struggle and of the Free Yemeni Movement asked Abdullah al-Wazir to join them in their scheme. They offered him the imamate upon the imam's death. Abdullah al-Wazir accepted.

Abdullah al-Wazir's claim to the imamate could not be disputed. He was a Zeidi, a Sayyid, and an intellectual, and he believed that he should succeed Yahya as imam. He had served the imam in senior military, administrative, and diplomatic functions before he was eased aside to make room for the imam's sons.[36]

Abdullah had been recalled to Sanaa as senior minister, and his brother Mohammed was appointed to take Abdullah's place in Damar. In Sanaa, Abdullah bought a large residence and expanded it by building an administrative annex from which he managed Damar through his brother. Abdullah also attended to administrative affairs which Imam Yahya assigned.

His stay in Sanaa at the side of the imam enhanced Abdullah's prestige and power. This facilitated the planning and execution of the assassination of Imam Yahya.

The conspirators drew a secret document that spelled out in detail their aims and desires upon the imam's death. The document was officially called the "National Holy Charter." It specified among its 39 articles that an imam shall be chosen who will be bound consultatively and constitutionally (Article 1L), that the Shari'a shall be inviolable (Article 3), and that a constitution for the land shall be drafted and presented to the imam for his opinion (Article 4). [37]

The charter was drawn in January 1948. In the same month, it became known to the imam, who immediately confronted Abdullah al-Wazir. The conciliatory tone of the imam was overshadowed by his action in summoning Prince Ahmad from Taiz to the capital to take charge of public affairs. The leaders of the conspiracy became afraid lest they be punished by Prince Ahmad.

In a hasty move, the conspirators decided to assassinate the imam and Prince Ahmad on the same day. On February 17, 1948, when Imam Yahya was on his way to his estate outside the capital accompanied by his prime minister, he was intercepted and shot. He and the prime minister were killed in a hail of bullets. Prince Ahmad received word of his father's assassination while on his way to the capital. He was also warned that the assassins were already stationed along his route waiting to intercept him. Ahmad immediately fled to Hajja and began to rally the tribes to his cause.

In Sanaa, two of Imam Yahya's sons were killed when they attempted to resist the coup. [38] However, the one person the conspirators wanted to kill managed to escape their trap.

THE 1948 COUP D'ETAT IS ABORTED

The leaders of the coup urged the people to accept Abdullah al-Wazir as Yahya's successor. They pressured many notables "to pay their fealty to Abdullah al Wazir." [39]

Al-Wazir's forces, which included members of the Society of Struggle, of the Free Yemeni Movement, and of the officer group, were under a great handicap in the ensuing struggle for power with Prince Ahmad. Prince Ahmad's cause was made easier by the facts that he fled to Hajja with enough money to distribute to the tribes and that his father had been cruelly assassinated. Declaring himself imam, Prince Ahmad invoked traditional tribal attachments by reminding the tribes that Imam Yahya, who was 83 years old and sick (he had become partially paralyzed) at the time of his death, had not been permitted to die naturally. By this method, Prince Ahmad was able to gain valued tribal support from the central and eastern hills regions.

The cause of Prince Ahmad was further helped by intra-Arab reluctance to become involved in the internal affairs of Yemen. The Arab states, acting through the Arab League, were moved to resolve the Yemeni dispute. League deliberations voiced a disinclination to intervene. Consequently, the dispatch of a delegation to Yemen was not made until two weeks after the coup. By then it had become apparent that Prince Ahmad was winning the struggle.

The reluctance of the Arab League to resolve the Yemeni power struggle can be understood in terms of which Arab faction in the League had the greater influence. In 1948, the Arab League was under the influence of the conservative regimes of King Farouk of Egypt, King Abdul Aziz of Saudi Arabia, and King Abdullah of Jordan. These monarchs opposed the usurpation of power by Abdullah al-Wazir. Syria and Lebanon were relatively sympathetic toward the coup, and Iraq was neutral.[40] The kings of Saudi Arabia, Egypt, and Jordan could not tolerate a regime created through a coup d'etat, however similar in form to the regime it was replacing. The success of any violent political movement implied a danger to their own political systems. Thus, when Abdullah al-Wazir sent word to King Abdul Aziz asking for recognition, the Saudi monarch sent back a stern negative reply.[41]

The delegation sent by the Arab League to Yemen did not reach Sanaa. On its way it stopped at Jeddah, Saudi Arabia. Prince Ahmad took the opportune moment to contact the Saudi monarch, requesting him to delay the departure of the delegation from his kingdom and asserting that he would soon enter Sanaa. King Abdul Aziz complied with his wish. Prince Ahmad sent another telegram to the Arab League warning against intervention and stating that he was on his way to recapture Sanaa. When word reached the army under al-Wazir of the impending arrival of tribes loyal to Prince Ahmad, it deserted him to fight on the side of Ahmad.

This change in the attitude of the army and the rank
and file was partly in expectation of material returns,
but mainly, it seems, resulted from a strong feeling
of reaction, following the atrocious murder of the late
Imam, which produced an attitude of apathy towards
a government which claimed to inaugurate a regime
of order and justice.[42]

A few days later al-Wazir was captured, and the coup d'etat was
ended.

In the aftermath of the coup, many people were executed
and many more fled the country into Aden and into other Arab
states to continue their resistance against the Hamid al-Din rule.
Abdullah al-Wazir; Ali al-Wazir, former governor of Taiz; Ahmad
al-Muta'a, founder of the Society of Struggle; and Hussein al-
Kibsi, former personal advisor to Imam Yahya, were beheaded.
Ahmad Numan, co-founder of the Free Yemeni Movement, was
jailed along with many other coup participants in the Hajja prison.

Although Prince Ahmad was able to regain political power,
with himself as imam, political discontent against his regime
intensified when political and economic reforms were not forthcoming. The problems that he faced were similar to those
encountered by his father. The only measurable difference
was that traditional values under Ahmad's reign were progressively losing ground to the forces of modernity, which were
being influenced by the changing political environment in the
Middle East.

NOTES

1. Amin al-Rayhani, Arabian Peak and Desert: Travels
in al-Yaman (London: Constable, 1930), p. 88.
2. Ibid.
3. A. Faroughy, Introducing Yemen (New York:
Orientalia, 1947), p. 24.
4. Ibrahim A. al-Wazir, Bein Yadai al-Ma'sah: Hadith ila
al-Yamani'in al-Na'zehin ("Between the Hands of Despair: A
Discourse to the Yemeni Emigrants") (Beirute: Daar al-Andalus,
1962), p. 64.
5. Ibid., p. 65.
6. Faroughy, Introducing Yemen, p. 23.
7. Ibid., p. 27.
8. Ahmad Zabarah, counselor to the Yemen embassy in
Washington, D.C. and former chargé d'affaires of the legation

of the Mutawakkilite Kingdom of Yemen in Washington, D.C., assured me that Yemen's national income could not have exceeded $10 million annually in the 1920s and 1930s because Yemen's resources were limited, and the regime of Imam Yahya depended only on revenues derived from the zakat and from taxes on imported and exported commodities, which were little. Personal interview, August 15, 1975.

9. Khari-din az-Zarkali, Shibhal Jazirah fi Ahad al-Malik Abdul Aziz ("Portrait of the (Arabian) Peninsula during the time of King Abdul Aziz") (Beirute: Matabe Dar al-Galum, 1970), vol. 2 of 4, pp. 635-36. Quoted from Bakor Kashmiri, Ibn Saud: The Arabian Nation Builder (Ph.D. dissertation, Howard University), Appendix XI, p. 258.

10. Richard Sanger, The Arabian Peninsula (New York: Cornell University Press, 1954), p. 111.

11. Amin al-Rayhani, Muluk al-Arab ("The Arab Kings") (Beirute: Daar al-Rayhani, 1960), pp. 78-79.

12. Abdul Allah A. al-Jirafi, al-Mugtadif min Ta'rikh al-Yaman ("Excerpts from the History of Yemen") (Cairo: Daar Ahya'e al-Kutub al-Arabiah, 1955), p. 227.

13. Robert Stookey, Political Change in Yemen: A Study of Values and Legitimacy (Ph.D. dissertation, University of Texas at Austin, 1972), p. 348.

14. al-Jirafi, al-Mugtadif min Ta'rikh, p. 233.

15. Abdullah al-Shamahi, Yaman: al-Insan wa al-Hadharah ("Yemen: Man and Civilization") (Yemen: Daar al-Hann lil-Taba'ah, 1972), p. 175.

16. Ibid., p. 176.

17. Stookey, Political Change in Yemen, p. 375.

18. Gilliam King, Imperial Outpost: Aden (London: Oxford University Press, 1964), pp. 70-80.

19. Majid Khadduri, "Coup and Counter-Coup in the Yaman 1948," International Affairs 27 (January 1952):59.

20. Ibid.

21. Ibid., p. 60.

22. Harold Ingrams, The Yemen: Imams, Rulers, and Revolutions (London: 1963), pp. 68-70.

23. Eric Macro, Yemen and the Western World Since 1957 (London: C. Hurst, 1968), p. 60.

24. Mohammed Khalil, The Arab States and the Arab League: A Documentary Record, vol. 2 (Beirute: Khayats, 1962), pp. 885-86.

25. Ibid., p. 886.

26. In an interview with Prince al-Hassan ibn Yahya, it was pointed out to the author that Imam Yahya had valid security

reasons for removing Ali al-Wazir from Taiz. First, Imam Yahya's son Ahmad brought to his father's attention evidence of communication between Ali and the British in Aden to exclude Taiz Province, of which Ali was governor, from British attack. Although Imam Yahya decided not to act on this, he was finally convinced that Ali should be transferred from Taiz when Ahmad produced a letter in Ali's own handwriting to Ali's contact with the Italian governor of Asmara. The letter contained a request for arms and instructions for their transport by sea to a place near Mocha.

As for Abdullah Al-Wazir, Prince al-Hassan claims that information was abundant concerning his immobilization of subordinates, his hiring of personnel to collect the zakat, and then his submission of falsified books to Sanaa. In addition, he had had a dispute with the administrator of Yarim, whom he had threatened. When Abdullah discovered that the administrator was on his way to Sanaa to expose Abdullah to the imam, Abdullah telegraphed orders for the interception and return of the administrator. However, the fugitive took a road other than the usual one. He reached Sanaa and presented evidence to Imam Yahya of Abdullah's mismanagement of government funds. (Interview by the author with Prince al-Hassan, July 1981.)

27. When Prince Faisal ibn Abdul Aziz of Saudi Arabia advanced into Tahama, all Yemeni troops and administrative personnel, including the imam's son Abdullah, governor of Hodeida, were ordered by the imam to retreat to the mountains. At the same time, Abdullah al-Wazir, on his way back from negotiations with the Saudis, was returning with the rest of the Yemeni delegation through Hodeida. The imam instructed him to remain in the town during the absence of its governor. When the situation returned to normal, the imam's son returned to his post and Abdullah al-Wazir was excused. Although some who were not familiar with the facts assumed that the imam placed his son in al-Wazir's post, the imam had never intended to install al-Wazir in Hodeida while Damar Province was overseen by the al-Wazir family.

28. Macro, Yemen and the Western World, p. 78.

29. al-Shamahi, Yaman: al-Insan wa al-Hadharah, pp. 175-76.

30. Ibid., p. 176.

31. Ibid., pp. 173-204.

32. Sanger, The Arabian Peninsula, pp. 266-68.

33. al-Shamahi, Yaman: al-Insan wa al-Hadharah, p. 191.

34. Ibid., p. 197.

35. Stookey, Political Change in Yemen, p. 383.

36. Ibid.

37. al-Shamahi, <u>Yaman: al-Insan wa al-Hadharah</u>, pp. 201-22.

38. Princes Hussein and Mohsin were shot outside the gates of the imam's house in Sanaa by guards loyal to the coup.

39. Khadduri, "Coup and Counter-Coup in the Yaman," p. 63.

40. Ibid., p. 66.

41. For a more detailed account of the reaction of the League of Arab States and of the coup d'etat, see al-Shamahi, <u>Yaman: al-Insan wa al-Hadharah</u>, pp. 225-76.

42. Khadduri, "Coup and Counter-Coup in the Yaman," p. 67.

PART II
Era of Economic and Political Transition

3

FACTORS THAT
INFLUENCED TRANSITION

All political systems react to external and internal stress and, by so doing, attempt to reassert the system equilibrium by adopting change. Each state must go through this process. However, the manner in which change is adopted reflects the continuity or dislocation of political systems.

In the 1950s, Yemen underwent such a change that was caused by external pressures and internal stresses. However, Yemen's seemingly shallow response to the external and internal demands led to the adoption of cosmetic political and economic changes. Change, however, was imperative lest the regime lose control. The Yemeni government response to change was determined by three forces, working independently as well as collectively to cause change: Arab nationalism and its impact, the issue of succession and reform, and the 1955 coup d'etat.

ARAB NATIONALISM AND ITS IMPACT

All types of nationalism are generative forces that impel the masses and nations to become politically conscious. Nationalism is:

> . . . both limited and unlimited, and exclusive and
> comprehensive. It is a dogma, an axiom, a stereo-
> type, and a hypothesis at the same time. It means
> different things to different people. It is original,
> national, and international. In spite of its unlimited
> potential, it may be stemmed entirely. It is some-

> thing in the West and something else in the Arab
> world. It is both hell and salvation. Like a funda-
> mental law, nationalism lends itself very easily to
> the recognized ends; almost everyone aspires at the
> endeared end of unity. Yet it lends itself little, if
> at all, to the means; when it comes to how to achieve
> unity, nationalism is a labyrinth . . . In its extreme
> form it may lead to war or even to the destruction
> of humanity. That is why it is hated in one place
> and loved in another . . . It is the embodiment of
> the conscience of each individual nation.[1]

"Nationalism is the principle political manifestation of social
change."[2] It attempts to correct the imbalances of social life
in societies and tries to rectify such imbalances by giving
status, either economic or social, to those who have attained
skill. As such, it attempts to be egalitarian—a movement highly
charged with emotions. Nationalism in its general form is a
sociopolitical concept that springs from unique cultural and
historical factors. "Nationalism binds together people who
possess common cultural, linguistic, historical, or geographical
characteristics or experiences and who give their loyalty to
the same political group."[3]

Arab nationalism is all of the above and more. It is a
movement aimed at creating independence and Arab unity. It
is the feeling and awareness of Arabism, and it reflects the will
to restore to wholeness what has been violated by history, ad-
versity, and accident.[4]

Although Arab nationalism arose in various Arab states—
Tunisian nationalism, Moroccan nationalism, Sudanese nationalism,
and Syrian nationalism—it had a common goal: unity. Basic
consistencies were expressed in a few goals upon which there
was general agreement: Arabism, independence, unity, reform,
and progress.[5] Arabism was interpreted by the Arabs as a
concept that "denotes the essence of being an Arab—the essence
of belonging to the Arab nation, possession of Arabic as the
mother tongue, the fact of having been born an Arab. . . ."[6]

Arab nationalism was, like most nationalisms, ambivalent.
The ambivalence was a direct result of the Western culture that
dominated and superimposed itself on the Arab people. Arab
nationalism arose for the primary purpose of freeing the Arab
world from the servitude of Western imperialism. Its conceptual
framework was to revitalize Arab culture and history. However,
the technologically and industrially superior Western culture
inspired in Arab nationalists a sense of admiration and a feeling

of revulsion. On the one hand, Arab nationalists viewed Western culture as a system to be emulated, while, on the other hand, they viewed it with distaste. It was Western imperialism that was responsible for the fragmentation of the Arab world, for the creation of artificial boundaries separating historically geographical and cultural units, and for creating divisions within the Arab political and ideological realms.

The concept of Arab unity implies that historically the Arab people were a united entity until historical circumstances and accidents fragmented that entity into several states. Arab unity was a part of the Arab awakening. According to Fayez A. Sayegh, the "idea of Arab unity was in fact implicit in the total concept of the Arab awakening."[7]

The impact of Arab nationalism was not strong in Yemen during the reign of Imam Yahya. However, during the reign of Imam Ahman (1948-62), Arab nationalism made remarkable inroads into Yemen. The regime was unable to stem its tide or to ignore it. Both Yahya and Ahmad were concerned about the presence of Great Britain in Aden and the protectorate. But while Yahya was only confronted with the presence of the British, Imam Ahmad was plagued by other forces that were regionally generated. Thus, while Imam Yahya joined the League of Arab States in 1945 to enlist Arab support in his struggle against Great Britain without the pressures of Arab nationalism, Imam Ahmad had to always consider the forces of Arab nationalism in his policy decisions. There is no doubt, however, that Imam Yahya was influenced by Arab sentiments when he joined the Arab League. He believed that Yemen was intrinsically attached to the other Arab states linguistically, historically, and culturally. However, the primary reason for his decision was to guarantee Arab support against British imperialism. Moreover, the imam was aware of the shortcomings of the Arab League, which was created as an association, not as a union. It was a:

> locus of relations among political beings, not a political being in itself; a coordinator, or an instrument of coordination, of the actions of members who had retained in their own hands the power to formulate policy and execute actions, not a planner, nor an actor in its own right; a forum for the exchange of views among sovereign states, but not vested with sovereignty nor empowered to wield delegated authority.[8]

Article 7 of the Pact of the League asserted that league decisions were only binding on those states that accepted them. Hence,

the league was stripped of all true authority. It afforded the
Arab states the opportunity to gather into one pan-Arab fold[9]
without seemingly jeopardizing their independence or freedom
to associate with other non-Arab states. It enhanced the Arab
feeling of oneness and helped to motivate the Arab states to
promote inter-Arab cultural and educational advancements.

The Arab League had the foresight to develop an equilibrium
between traditionalism and modernity. It stressed an interest
in readjusting traditional Islam to Western technical and scientific
achievements,[10] and it has been credited with motivating the
Arabs to look toward a supranational Arab entity.[11] In international affairs, the Arab states have functioned, in more cases
than not, as an entity, and the league was instrumental in uniting
the Arab states on matters important to Arabism.

Similarly, Imam Yahya joined the United Nations in 1947.
He was not as concerned with Arab nationalism as he was with
British imperialism. The imam became convinced that joining
the United Nations would help to guarantee his southern borders
against British incursions.

The 1948 coup d'etat, although it failed, forced many
Yemeni reform-minded individuals to flee to Egypt. Their activities and their political ideas were not permitted to be publicized
until the Egyptian Revolution in 1952, specifically until Nasser
came to power in 1954. 1954 could be considered the year Arab
nationalism was revitalized, in the person of Gamal Abdul Nasser.

Nasser's political aspiration was to see the Arab world free
of foreign domination and influence. He promoted Arab "neutrality" by extricating himself from exclusive dependence upon the
Western powers. Arab "neutralism" was unique in that it asserted
its independence from both power blocs, Eastern as well as
Western. It was aimed at cultivating existing Arab relations
with all powers and at developing new relations, freely concluded,
mutually defined, and reciprocally implemented.[12]

Arab nationalists, imbued with a new spirit, assembled
around the political banner of Nasser. He had within a short
time established Egypt as an intrinsic part of the Arab world
and had politically and actively removed Egypt from the political
and economic influence of the Western powers. Furthermore,
he pursued the Arab struggle for independence. The Egyptian
government radio, "Voice of the Arabs," began encouraging
the Arab masses to free themselves from the servitude of imperialism. Egyptian money and arms were available to Arab
liberation movements from Aden to Algeria. President Nasser
made special efforts to evict the British from south Arabia.
Thus, "the problem of South Arabia became an all-Arab national

cause which Egypt sponsored and exploited with her great propaganda machine."[13] Consequently, Arab nationalism became identified with the new force of Nasserism.

The impact of Arab nationalism on Yemen became more powerful after 1954. In 1954, members of the Free Yemeni Movement in Egypt were permitted to publish political commentaries criticizing the Yemeni regime for its lack of reform. The effect of the broadcasts was indeed minimal, since radios in Yemen were only available to well-to-do families. However, with the introduction of the transistor into Yemen in 1955, the number of Yemenis who became attuned to the "Voice of the Arabs" increased twofold. Yemeni merchants, carpenters, and government workers became politically aware of events not only in the Arab world but also around the globe. The Yemeni, for the first time, began identifying with Arabs in Egypt, Syria, Algeria, and the Sudan. Such identification became manifestly apparent during the Suez War in 1956. Many Yemenis showed their sentiments to Egypt by demonstrating outside the British legation in Sanaa. Many others demanded to be sent to Egypt to fight alongside their Egyptian counterparts. Such sentiments clearly indicated that Arab nationalism had reached Bab al-Mandab.

The invasion of Egypt by Britain, France, and Israel was construed by the Arab world as an invasion against the entire Arab people. It was an Arab war felt in all the Arab capitals. The Suez War made President Nasser more popular among the Arab masses. It also stamped mass Arab approval on the political, social, and economic actions of the Egyptian Revolution, which, according to Tarequ Y. Ismael:

> Destroyed the feudal monarchical rule of Farouk,
> rid Egypt of British colonialism, instituted pro-
> grams for agricultural reform, liberated the Suez
> Canal from international monopolies, ended foreign
> control of Egyptian banks and companies, national-
> ized interests of large national capitalists, funded
> the public sector in the economy and public owner-
> ship of the major means of production, and, finally,
> undertook a large movement for industrialization
> and the building of the Aswan Dam—these were
> accomplishments that had profound impact on the
> level of consciousness, attitudes and behavior of
> the Egyptian as well as the larger Arab masses.[14]

The regime of Imam Ahmad was not altogether unresponsive to Arab nationalism. The imam, in response to Arab nationalism,

sent a delegation to the 1955 Bandung Conference on nonaligned
nations. Along with Egypt, Yemen established links of communication with the Socialist bloc countries. Such links led to the
establishment of diplomatic relations between Yemen and the
Soviet Union in the latter part of 1955 and between Yemen and
the People's Democratic Republic of China in 1956. Also in 1956,
the imam went to Saudi Arabia to sign the Jeddah Military Pact
with Egypt and Saudi Arabia. The pact aligned Yemen with
Egypt and opened the door for increased cooperation between
traditionalist Yemen and revolutionary Egypt. This alignment
was followed in 1958 by the creation of the United Arab States,
which confederated Yemen with the United Arab Republic
(U.A.R.). Yemen's association with the U.A.R. placed it in
the forefront of Arab nationalism. Yemen was no longer declared
anachronistic, reactionary, and stagnant. To the Arabs, the
imam had assumed a leadership role in the promotion and promul-
gation of Arab nationalism.

During the years 1955-62, Yemen was penetrated by more
foreigners than ever before. Egyptians, Russians, Americans,
Chinese, Germans, and Czechs entered Yemen either to undertake diplomatic missions, to train the Yemeni army, or to help
the Yemeni government improve the economic conditions of the
state. Others also made their way into Yemen in search of geo-
logical and archaeological finds. This development, reinforced
by Arab nationalism, encouraged the Yemeni regime to move
toward internationalism. Yemeni missions were opened in most
West European capitals as well as in the Socialist Bloc countries.
The continued presence of the British in South Arabia contributed
to Yemen's international involvement.

Internally, the Yemeni people were being politicized from
abroad. The transistor became the primary vehicle for the
political indoctrination of the Yemeni masses. Political terminolo-
gies, often heard in propaganda commentaries over the "Voice
of the Arabs," became a part of the common Yemeni vocabulary.
The Yemeni began using the terms Arab nationalism (al-qawmiyyah
al-arabiyyah), dictatorship (al-dictatoriyyah), Arabism (al-
urubah), political tyranny (al-istibdad al-siyasi), freedom
(al-huriyah), imperialism (istimar), feudalism (al-iqtaiyyah),
revolution (al-thawrah), and anti-Arabism (shuubiyyah) without a general understanding of their meanings or their ramifications. To the average Yemeni, the use of such terms implied
intellectualism and an awareness of political events.

In the three years (1958-61) during which Yemen was confederated with the United Arab Republic, the "Voice of the
Arabs" rarely, if ever, attacked the imamate regime. But when

the United Arab States was terminated in 1961, the fury of the "Voice of the Arabs" was directed against the imamate, specifically against the imam. Egyptian broadcasts identified the imam as a puppet of imperialism and as a reactionary working against Arabism and Arab nationalism.

The Egyptian authorities, moreover, permitted Mohammed Zubeiri, co-founder of the Free Yemeni Movement, to broadcast directly into Yemen. Zubeiri's political commentaries had a far-reaching impact on the Yemeni people. Speaking in Yemeni dialect and recognized as a Yemeni, his broadcasts became popular among the Yemenis. Zubeiri attacked the corruption of the imamate and directly accused the imam of political tyranny. His commentaries had an unstablizing effect on the Yemeni society. Demonstrations against the imamate regime erupted in Sanaa and Taiz.

The Egyptian government, not completely satisfied with Zubeiri's political attacks on the imamate regime, proceeded to impose Abdurrahman Beidhani as the "chief spokesman" of the Free Yemenis in Egypt. Beidhani's credentials as a Yemeni were suspect. His father was Indian, and he had been raised in Egypt.

Beidhani was permitted by the Egyptian authorities to broadcast into Yemen through the "Voice of the Arabs," and he was allowed to write the political intentions of the Free Yemenis in the Egyptian weekly official organ, Rose el-Youssef.[15]

Unlike Zubeiri, Beidhani attacked the Hashemites (descendants of the Prophet Mohammed) and accused them of political oppression and nepotism. He called for either their eviction from Yemen or for their destruction. Beidhani imbued Rose el-Youssef with a vehemence that even Zubeiri questioned.[16] To Beidhani, the only way the Shaf'is could rid themselves of the Hashemites was through a violent revolution. As the representative of the Free Yemenis, Beidhani demanded the destruction of the imamate institution, the extermination of the Sayyids, and the birth of a republic excluding the Sayyids. His articles preached the necessity of dividing the state into two political units, one Shaf'i and the other Zeidi. In essence, Beidhani called for the partitioning of the Yemeni society along sectarian lines.

Beidhani's virulent attacks on the Hashemites raised the ire of Zubeiri, who contended that, had it not been for the Hashemites, Yemen's independence would not have materialized. Moreover, he said their nationalism could not be questioned: they were Yemenis whose principles were derived from the Prophet, and, like the Shaf'is, their origin stemmed from the

Himyarites,[17] not from Zeidism or Shaf'ism. He wrote, "The
Hashemites are blessed . . . They are our brothers not our
masters . . . Our land is their land, and we and they share
equally in the good."[18]

The Egyptian propaganda against the imamate regime was
effective in destabilizing the Yemeni society. It helped to pave
the road for the revolution. The imam found it beyond his physical power to stop revolutionary ideas from penetrating Yemen
through the air waves. The ideas of Arab nationalism and Arabism were superimposing themselves on the Yemeni society.

ISSUES OF SUCCESSION AND REFORM

The Yemeni nationalists, exemplified by the Free Yemenis,
were inspired by the ideals of Arab nationalism. They were
determined individuals who desired to reform Yemeni society
along the lines of economic, social, and political development.
Initially, they favored a political objective that would be favorable to change. They adopted a plan aimed at destabilizing the
royal family by dividing it into two factions and at ensuring
political change by weakening the conservative Zeidi power.
The implementation of the Free Yemenis plan surfaced as early
as 1951, when the issue of succession was brought to the imam's
attention by Ahmad Numan, Ahmad al-Shami, and Abdul Rahman
al-Iryani.[19] All wanted to see the imam's son, Mohammed al-
Badr, named crown prince. Al-Badr's political liberalism and
his trust in reform-minded Yemenis won him the political support
of the Free Yemenis. The Free Yemenis congregated around him
and adopted several objectives aimed at advancing their cause
while promoting friction within the royal family. Their objectives
were to convince the imam that the imamate should remain within
the Hamid al-Din family on the condition that it be bestowed on
al-Badr, the most loyal and trusted of the royal family; to convince the imam to curb the political antagonism of his brothers
toward the Free Yemenis; to convince al-Badr to persuade his
father to accept Egyptian assistance; and to persuade the imam
that the Free Yemenis still in jail be freed to serve as soldiers
of al-Badr.[20] These objectives were adopted in 1952.

On the issue of succession, Imam Ahmad's political acumen
seemed to have deserted him. He believed that his brother,
al-Hassan, was more deserving to succeed him, since al-Hassan
was the most likely individual from the royal family to receive
Zeidi acceptance. But Ahmad favored the succession of his son,
even though al-Badr's qualifications were questionable under

Zeidi doctrine. Al-Badr had no real grasp of Zeidi law, his
style of living was rather unconventional in Zeidi terms, and
he embraced liberal ideas that conflicted with conservative Zeidi
traditions.[21] Therefore, al-Badr was considered an unlikely
imam by the Zeidis.[22]

The problem of succession had effects similar to those
during the reign of Imam Yahya: "the increase of factionalism
within the royal family, the dissatisfaction of the conservative
ulema, and the alienation of ambitious or conservative Sayyids."[23]

Strong opposition to Imam Ahmad's attempt to implement
the new ideas of primogeniture came primarily from his conservative brothers, principally from Abdullah, Abbas, and al-Hassan.[24]
They viewed the imam's move as contrary to Zeidi law. Thus,
a conflict developed between the imam and them. It was reported
by a critic of the imamate that the imam believed that his brothers
were plotting to assassinate him.[25] Undoubtedly, the inability
of the royal family to compromise on the issue of succession
helped to promote the final schism in the royal family.

The issue of succession was compounded by the increasing
demand for reform from among both the Free Yemenis and the
young, educated Yemenis who had studied abroad.[26] Many of
the latter had returned to Yemen with a feeling of achievement,
and they were eager to put their skills into the service of the
state. However, they were not given their due share of responsibility in the administration of the government, largely because
the system could not absorb them. They found the country
essentially the same as it had been when they had gone abroad.
There were no paved roads, no modern communication systems,
and no tangible economic developments. The whole system
revolved around the person of the imam, and nothing could be
done or implemented without his expressed approval. The imam's
authority was felt throughout the political, social, and economic
systems, and since the imam seemed unwilling to move in the
direction of reform, the entire system appeared inert. Finding
the state to be so archaic, the young, educated Yemenis became
discontented.[27] They were embarrassed to see the backwardness of their country in comparison with other Arab states. A
few, therefore, openly defected by quietly slipping into Aden
to join the Free Yemenis.[28]

The imam's lack of responsiveness to political, economic,
and social reforms may be explained in terms of the struggle
for power between the traditionalist and the modernist (reformer).
Each attempted to supplant the other. The traditionalist, recognizing that his powers (political, economic, and social) are
derived from his acceptance of traditional values, fights to

preserve those values. They are familiar to him, hence they
are to be tolerated and maintained. Those values unfamiliar to
him, even though they may be virtuous, cannot be tolerated.[29]
The modernist, feeling a sense of intellectual arrogance, cannot
tolerate values that do not correspond to his thinking. He
thinks in terms of the good of the "whole," and he believes
that he is more able to satisfy the need of the "whole" than
could a traditionalist. In this sense, the traditionalist and the
modernist are polarized. In actuality, however, the traditionalist
derives his powers from traditional values (Islamic or non-Islamic).
His powers are legitimately based on traditionalism and cultural
beliefs. The modernist, feeling hemmed in, claims the traditionalist is unoriginal, noninnovative, and stagnant. Change, to him,
can only come when the traditionalist bases his legitimacy upon
the wishes of the masses.

The Arab modernist, including the Yemeni modernist, was
indifferent to the theory that the older the society the greater
the stability and the less its institutions need reform.[30] The
Yemeni institution of the imamate, having endured for centuries,
was stable and tolerant of reforms. But the demands for change
made by the Yemeni modernist were not gradual, were often
antiestablishment, and were indifferent to the absence of economic resources in Yemen. The latter factor is of immense
importance in attempts by a traditionalist state to reform. Saudi
Arabia, where the Islamic tradition is very much in control, is
in a state of social and political stability largely because its
resources are sufficient to satisfy the modernist demand for
reform. The Saudi family controls the administration of the
government, but it permits the government to be staffed with
Saudis trained and educated abroad. The government, therefore, not only satisfies the immediate needs of foreign-educated
Saudis by employing them, but it also satisfies their psychological
need for acceptance. Thus, harmony is achieved between the
traditionalist and the modernist.

In Yemen, the inability of the regime to satisfy those needs
of the Yemeni modernist resulted in widening the schism between
the traditionalist and the modernist. Thus, the modernist
attempted to displace the traditionalist, while the traditionalist
tried to rule the modernist.

In both cases, foreign ideas were absorbed. With regard
to Saudi Arabia, the foreign element worked in harmony with
both the modernist and the traditionalist. The traditionalist
used the foreign component to help in attempts to reform. The
foreign element was willing to assist the traditionalist lest it
lose its valuable economic interests in the state. Thus, the

Arabian-American Oil Company (ARAMCO) assisted the Saudi regime in sending Saudi students abroad for higher education at its own expense. It followed by guaranteeing them positions in the company tantamount to their educational achievements. The economic interests of both the Saudi government and of ARAMCO were satisfied. Cooperation between the traditionalist element and the foreign entity helped to satisfy the demands for change and reform.

The Yemeni regime also attempted to use the assistance of foreign entities. Many foreign countries accepted Yemeni students and paid their education expenses. However, Yemen possessed no valuable economic resources in which the foreign entity had an interest. Foreign investments in Yemen, therefore, were minimal. Cooperation between the traditionalist and the foreign element in Yemen was missing.

The conflict between the traditionalist and the modernist in Yemen was also apparent in the army. Imam Ahmad, like his father, was caught between his desire to modernize the army and his wish to keep modern ideas away from his domain. The imam was apprehensive about the small Yemeni officer group that had come into contact with new ideas and methods during foreign training. It was manifestly apparent to him that this group represented a new elite in Yemen, an elite whose political, economic, and social notions ran contrary to his own. The imam suspected that the officer group might support attempts to change the political structure in Yemen, since the officers were consciously aware of the political forces both in the Arab world and in Yemen. He, therefore, chose to inhibit the development of a strong Yemeni army. More specifically, the imam chose to rely on the tribes to ensure security, which was an attempt to preserve traditional values. The tribes had reinstated the Hamid al-Din rule in 1948 and had helped to preserve the imamate throughout the centuries.

THE COUP D'ETAT OF 1955

The coup d'etat of 1955 was led by Prince Abdullah, the imam's foreign minister. Abdullah had travelled extensively, was known to be pro-Western, and favored closer ties with both the United States and Great Britain.

The coup occurred as a result of a dispute between a group of Yemeni soldiers and residents of a village in the north region of al-Hawban, north of Taiz. The dispute resulted in the death of two soldiers, who were later revenged by their compatriots.

This incident was probably undertaken with the approval of Colonel Ahmad al-Thilayya, who was jailed by the imam for his role in the 1948 coup d'etat, was later released as a sign of reconciliation, and was given the duty of training the Yemeni army. He was a member of the Free Yemenis and a supporter of Prince Abdullah.

After the soldiers took their revenge on the village of al-Hawban, they turned against the imam, demanding his abdication from the imamate. Loyal to Prince Abdullah, the soldiers surrounded the imam's palace. Prince Abdullah summoned the ulema and asked for their allegiance. However, a great many of the ulema and notables hesitated in giving him their allegiance for fear of violating their previous oaths to Imam Ahmad. Prince Abdullah thereupon sent a delegation to the imam to ask for his resignation. The imam wrote an ambiguous statement that indicated the "forfeiture of work," but he never mentioned abdication from the imamate. [31] The statement was phrased to confuse the delegation and to delay the ulema from arriving at a decision.

When word reached al-Badr of his father's dilemma, [32] he immediately went to Hajja to gather support for his besieged father from the Hashid and Bakkil tribes. These were the same tribes that had supported the imam in the coup d'etat of 1948. When word reached the 600 soldiers in Taiz of the impending arrival of 8,000 tribal warriors, resistance began to dissipate. Soon the rebellious soldiers dispersed, and the leaders of the coup were caught and executed. Two members of the royal family were also executed, Prince Abdullah and Prince Abbas. The latter had supported the coup from Sanaa and had been appointed by Prince Abdullah as his prime minister.

The 1955 coup weakened, divided, and crippled the royal family. Not only were two members of the family executed, but the imam removed his other brothers from the mainstream of government affairs. [33] In 1956, the imam recognized that the Free Yemenis had conspired to incite friction between him and his brothers by insisting that al-Badr be declared crown prince. The imam told Ahmad Numan, co-founder of the Free Yemeni Movement, "Do you want me to speak bluntly . . . ? By God! You and al-Iryani (another leading member of the Free Yemenis) are the head of this dilemma . . . I used to tell you: 'It is not time to consider the issue of the Crown Prince,' but you disagreed." [34]

In many ways, the 1955 coup was similar to the coup of 1948. The motive in both cases was the desire for reform and the presence of rivals anxious to take the place of the legal ruler. However, the army was the focal instrument of the 1955 coup from the beginning to the end. The failure of both coups can be attributed to the same factors: the inadequacy of the armed forces at the disposal of the rebels as compared with the overwhelming tribal forces supporting the ruling imam, the questionable allegiance of the ulema and notables of the community to the usurpers, and the lack of mass support for the action of the rebels.[35] Moreover, neither coup was interested in breaching the legal continuity of government or in completely transforming it, but rather supported transferring the legal authority from one hand to another while maintaining the traditional Zeidi values and rules. Unlike its predecessor, the 1955 coup split the Free Yemenis into two factions: one supporting al-Badr and the other supporting Prince Abdullah. Furthermore, the 1955 coup differed from its predecessor in that the 1948 coup was composed of Yemeni intellectuals who saw in the continuation of the Hamid al-Din's authority a rule associated with despotism and tyranny. They wished to make the imamate more responsive to the demands of the people rather than to the wishes of the ruler. The National Holy Charter was indicative of their political philosophy and reformist tendencies.

The 1955 coup received similar attention from the Arab states as had its predecessor. The Arab states were, in general, indifferent to the coup. Egypt showed greater interest in its development than any other Arab state.

In concert with many of the Free Yemenis, Egypt rejected the coup and acted to prevent its success. Mohammed Zubeiri was permitted to broadcast through the "Voice of the Arabs" an appeal to the Yemenis to quell the insurrectionists. Zubeiri and his followers, along with Nasser, could not accept what they believed to be Prince Abdullah's pro-Western attitudes. He was accused of being a puppet of the West. The effectiveness of Zubeiri's broadcasts is still unclear. Nevertheless, it can be surmised that Zuebiri's political opposition to Prince Abdullah did not imply acceptance of Imam Ahmad. He and the Egyptian government rejected Abdullah in favor of al-Badr. Prince Abdullah had shown an independent political mind, which the Free Yemenis had believed could not be easily influenced. Moreover, he had been one of the conservative royal princes who opposed leniency to political prisoners. Al-Badr, on the other hand, was believed to be susceptible to political influence, and the Free Yemenis had taken great pains to win his support.

NOTES

1. Mohammed M. H. Shehab Eddin, Pan-Arabism and the Islamic Tradition (Ph.D. dissertation, American University, Washington, D.C., 1966), pp. 212-13.

2. Manfred Halpern, The Politics of Social Change in the Middle East and North Africa (Princeton: Princeton University Press, 1963), p. 197.

3. Jack Plano and Milton Greenberg, The American Political Dictionary (New York: Holt, Rinehart & Winston, 1963), p. 11.

4. Hisham Sharabi, Nationalism and Revolution in the Arab World (New York: Van Nostrand, 1966), p. 97.

5. Charles D. Cremeans, The Arabs and the World (New York: Praeger, 1963), p. 57.

6. Sharabi, Nationalism and Revolution, p. 96.

7. Fayez A. Sayegh, Arab Unity (New York: Devin-Adair, 1958), p. 7.

8. Ibid., p. 129.

9. Ibid., p. 139.

10. B. Y. Boutros-Ghali, "The Arab League: 1945-1955," International Conciliation (May 1954):442.

11. Jacques Berque, The Arabs: Their History and Future (London: Faber and Faber, 1964), p. 250.

12. Sayegh, Arab Unity, p. 177.

13. George Haddad, Revolution and Military Rule in the Middle East: The Arab States; Part II: Egypt, the Sudan, Yemen, and Libya, vol. 3 (Santa Barbara: University of California Press, 1973), p. 231.

14. Tarequ Y. Ismael, "The Rejection of Western Models of Government in the Arab World: The Case of Nasserism" (University of Calgary, Calgary, Canada) (Delivered at the 1975 annual meeting of the American Political Science Association, San Francisco, September 2-5, 1975), p. 5.

15. Beidhani's column first appeared in Rose el-Youssef under the title "Secrets of Yemen" on January 22, 1962, exactly 25 days after the termination of the United Arab States.

16. Ahmad Zabarah emphasized to me that friction between Zubeiri and Beidhani surfaced as a consequence of Beidhani's political rhetoric attacking the Hashemites. Zubeiri believed that such attacks were nonproductive and defeatist in essence. Zubeiri asserted that the Free Yemenis were struggling against the political tyrany of the imam, not against the Hashemites. Zabarah emphasized that Zubeiri once declared to Beidhani, "If you are fighting the Hashemites, then I am with them." Personal interview, September 15, 1975.

17. The Himyarit civilization flourished in Yemen from 115 B.C. until 525 A.D.

18. Ahmad Mohammed al-Shami, Min al-Adab al-Yamani ("From the Literature of Yemen") (Beirute: Matba'at al-Shuruq, 1974), p. 100.

19. Ahmad Numan, Ahmad al-Shami, and Abdul Rahman al-Iryani were jailed by Imam Ahmad for their roles in the 1948 coup d'etat. All three were able to establish a line of communication with the imam and al-Badr during their jail terms. Abdullah al-Shamahi, Yaman: al-Insan wa al-Hadharah ("Yemen: Man and Civilization") (Yemen: Daar al-Haan lil-Taba'ah, 1972), p. 181.

20. Mohammed Ahmad Numan, al-Atraf al-Ma'aniah ("The Concerned Parties") (Aden: Al-Sabban wa Shuraka'hu, 1965), pp. 65-67.

21. Robert Stookey, Political Change in Yemen: A Study of Values and Legitimacy (Ph.D. dissertation, University of Texas at Austin, 1972), p. 384.

22. Haddad, Revolution and Military Rule in the Middle East, p. 273.

23. Robert Stookey, Political Change in Yemen, p. 384.

24. Numan, al-Atraf al-Ma'aniah, pp. 65-66.

25. al-Shamahi, Yaman: al-Insan wa al-Hadharah, p. 280.

26. William Brown, "The Yemeni Dilemma," Middle East Journal 17 (Autumn 1963):349-67, reports that by 1961 there were from 300 to 400 Yemenis in Egyptian secondary schools, more than 100 at Cairo University, and an additional 70 to 80 in European and U.S. educational institutions.

27. Ibid., pp. 354-55.

28. Edgar O'Ballance, The War in the Yemen (Hamden, Conn.: Archon, 1971), p. 51.

29. Monroe Berger, The Arab World Today (New York: Doubleday, 1964), p. 178.

30. Hamilton A. R. Gibb, "Social Reform: Factor X," Perspective of the Arab World, an Atlantic Monthly Supplement (1956):17.

31. The text of the imam's statement of abdication can be found in al-Shamahi, Yaman: al-Insan wa al-Hadharah, p. 334.

32. Al-Badr was warned of his father's dilemma by Ahmad al-Shami and Ahmad Numan, who had been sent to Hodeida by Prince Abdullah to place al-Badr under security. Both al-Shami and Numan had recently been released from the Hajja prison by the imam as a sign of reconciliation.

33. Numan, al-Atraf al-Ma'aniah, p. 70.

34. Ibid., pp. 72-73.

35. Haddad, Revolution and Military Rule in the Middle East, p. 236.

4

REGIONAL POLITICS

Imam Yahya's foreign policy of strict isolationism was altered by Imam Ahmad in order to placate the forces pressing on his regime and to preserve the imamate institution. The coup d'etat of 1955 was instrumental in convincing the imam to reconcile his differences with the Free Yemeni Movement and to improve his relationship with the Arab states. No longer was isolationism a satisfactory policy in the ever changing Middle East. New initiatives were required, which were made imperative by the demands of Arab nationalism.

Recognizing the potential dangers to his regime, Imam Ahmad improved his relationship with the Arab states. The intention of this chapter is to discuss Yemen's regional political policies and to assess their results. This chapter is concerned with the Jeddah Military Pact among Yemen, Egypt, and Saudi Arabia, the confederation between Yemen and the United Arab Republic (U.A.R.), and the dismemberment of the confederation. However, before the imam's regional politics are evaluated, it is essential to consider the concept of coherence and incoherence,[1] as developed by Manfred Halpern. In this discussion, however, Halpern's theory on incoherence is limited to evaluating the concept of incoherence in its relationship to the policy of isolationism as adopted by Imam Yahya.

Briefly stated, Halpern asserts that "the world is being molded neither by a conspiracy of world revolutionaries nor by counter-revolutionaries . . . but primarily by unintended, incoherent change."[2] Incoherence to Halpern means "the break in the links between individuals, groups, and concepts which give men the capacity to cope with continuity and change, with collaboration and conflict, and justice."[3]

Halpern's hypothesis emphasizes that in every society and in all recorded history encounters exist between sets of polarities of different types that give individuals the capacity to deal simultaneously with continuity and change, collaboration and conflict, and justice.[4] According to him, whenever a break occurs in the function of one or more polarities, incoherence emerges. Resorting to another polarity or polarities becomes essential to reestablishing coherency in the system. This development is unintended and basically accidental.

Since this discussion will be limited to evaluating the concept of incoherence in its relationship to the policy of isolationism in Yemen, incoherence becomes loosely defined as contradition.

Isolation, as defined by Halpern, is a relationship in which:

> individuals and groups reciprocally agree upon one mode of collaboration—to refrain from demanding anything of each other. . . . This requires for the sake of continuity the avoidance of all direct conflict intended to lead to change in, with, or by the other.[5]

In view of this definition, it becomes immediately apparent that incoherence in the Yemeni formulation of isolationism was imminent. The imamate government adopted isolationism unilaterally. There was no prior agreement between Yemen and other states. Adherence to and respect for isolationism by other groups or individuals is required in order for it to be effective. The world was neither willing to tolerate Yemen's isolationism nor did it intend to permit Yemen to remain apart from it. Foreign states, as previously noted, tried to establish economic and political interests in Yemen. Italy and the Soviet Union were able to induce Yemen to establish treaties of friendship and commerce with them. Yemen was also persuaded to permit Italian and Soviet doctors as well as foreign manufactured goods into the state. Consequently, foreign ideas were introduced, and an antithesis was interposed into the Yemeni society. Initially, this antithesis had a minimal effect on Yemeni traditional values and beliefs, but its growth was inevitable.

The greatest contributor to the development of incoherence in Yemen came as a direct result of the imamate's policy toward Great Britain in Aden and the protectorate. Imam Yahya's insecurity about the presence of Great Britain on his southern borders was instrumental in convincing him to modernize his army. He not only purchased Italian arms but also sent a mission of young Yemeni cadets to the Baghdad Military Academy in 1936 for training and education. However, the imam's apprehensions about foreign ideas prompted him to recall the mission prior to its intended completion. The recall of the cadets reflected the imam's cognizance of the fact that foreign ideas represented a danger to his nation's traditional systems. Similarly, he showed that same cognizance of danger when he invited an Iraqi military mission to Yemen. The imam cut short its stay because the members of the mission were spreading ideas construed by the regime as alien and threatening. This example is significant because it illustrates the inability of the regime to maintain itself aloof from international involvement while attempting to alleviate its insecurity in the face of British presence in Aden. It is also significant because it contributed to increasing the cleavage between the established thesis (traditionalism) and the new antithesis (modern ideas).

Incoherence also increased as a result of the economic conditions of Yemen. Since many Yemenis derived their livelihood from the land, it became exceedingly difficult for them to improve their meager living. The exacting economic conditions literally forced many Yemenis to emigrate to Aden, Ethiopia, the Sudan, other Arab states, or to other areas in the world. Yemeni emigrants kept in constant contact with Yemen by sending money to their families and by periodically visiting their homeland. They thus became another source channeling modern ideas into Yemen. Moreover, as previously discussed, the Yemenis in the Tihama region conducted extensive commerce with areas adjacent to Yemen. Their contacts with the outside world became another channel of modern ideas into Yemen. Through the Yemeni emigrant and the Yemeni commercial entrepreneur, modern ideas were reaching not only city dwellers but also the tribes. Consequently, the thesis/antithesis conflict was intensified and extended to rural areas.

Up until 1944, incoherence in Yemen had not begun to assert itself in outright and articulate criticism of the regime. The creation of the Free Yemeni Movement in that year indicated that incoherence had reached a level dangerous to the ruling family but not to the imamate. This was manifestly apparent, first in the formulation by the Free Yemenis of the National Holy Charter, which detailed their political aims and goals. The fact that the charter called for the establishment of a constitution that would legally specify the duties of the imam clearly indicated an extension of contradiction to traditionally (not Islamic) accepted practices. The arbitrary rule of the imam was now questioned. Second, the Free Yemenis indicated their support of the imamate as an accepted institution when they chose a Sayyid and an avowed supporter of the imamate, Abdullah

al-Wazir, to be the next imam. The Free Yemenis were not
working for the abolishment of the imamate. Rather they were
reform-minded individuals who wanted to see reforms in the
political, economic, and social sectors of the state.

The coup d'etat of 1948 was initiated to replace the ruling
Hamid al-Din family. Ideology played little or no role in the
rivalry. Personal claims differed between the insurrectionists
and the ruling family. Personal sentiments and ideas conflicted.
Thus, the insurrectionists wished to open the country to the
outside world while preserving traditional institutions, but the
ruling family wanted to import modern technologies without becoming internationally involved. One wanted to see reforms
instituted, while the other was reluctant to pursue reforms lest
political authority be lost.

Up until 1948, incoherence had been kept relatively under
control. But, specifically after the loss of Palestine to Zionism
in 1948 and the reemergence of Arab nationalism, the regime
had greater difficulty in coping with the contradiction. Arab
nationalism and all that it implied introduced into Yemen new
elements that manifested themselves in the development and
extension of incoherence.

Like his father, Imam Ahmad sought to import modern technology into his country while preserving the conservative traditional system. His task, however, was more difficult. The
forces of modernity were supplanting many traditional patterns
and values. The greatest contributor to the growth of incoherence in the 1950s was education. In this context, education
means political indoctrination, contacts with the outside world,
and association.

As previously stated, the Yemeni was being politically
indoctrinated through the "Voice of the Arabs." Such indoctrination helped to dilute the principle of emanation. According
to Halpern, emanation is that concept by which:

> (1) one treats the other solely as an extension of
> one's personality, one's own will and power—as an
> embodiment of one's self—and (2) the other accepts
> his denial of a separate identity as legitimate be-
> cause of the mysterious source of nature of the
> overwhelming power of the other. [6]

Emanation was clearly apparent in the Yemeni society from the
time of Imam Yahya ibn al-Hussein. The Yemenis believed that
the imams, as descendants of the Prophet Mohammed, were
blessed. Their spiritual purity was beyond reproach. The
imams came to personify the personality of their subjects, who

believed them to possess abstract, spiritual powers. As late as the 1950s, many tribes believed that Imam Ahmad could not be killed by a bullet because, through the power of God, it would change into a soft, pliable object upon impact. Emanation, therefore, was helpful in controlling tribal discord.

Emanation as a source of stability was being further weakened by Yemeni students going abroad for higher education. By coming in direct contact with other societies and other ideas, the students became more aware of the shortcomings of their own society. Many of the students, moreover, established direct contact with Mohammed Zubeiri in Cairo. His influence on them can only be conjectured, but it is safe to surmise that he was not only respected for his intellect but also for his political activism. Upon the return of the Yemeni graduates to Yemen, they found the state to be essentially the same as it had been when they had left. Consequently, many of them became opponents of the regime. Traditional values were construed as archaic. The Free Yemenis were instrumental in smuggling into Yemen pamphlets, books, and newspapers critical of the imam. The fact that criticism of the regime was now being articulated by many Yemenis served as another source in the augmentation of incoherence.

The coup d'etat of 1955 illustrated how far the struggle between modernity and traditionalism had progressed. The coup was significant because it was aborted with the help of the Free Yemenis. The fact that the Free Yemenis were split in their support of the coup illustrated that they still possessed no formulated ideology or political program. They had political concepts that could not be translated into a political program. Therefore, their sentiments were declared either for Prince Abdullah (the conservative-minded) or for Crown Prince al-Badr (the reform-minded). However, since most of them supported al-Badr, their political position was markedly improved. Future decisions by the regime reflected their political aspirations. But the coherence (stability) that was restored after the coup was only temporary.

In sum, incoherence developed in Yemen because the imam's goals conflicted with their means in achieving those goals. This same conflict was manifestly apparent in Imam Ahmad's regional politics initiated after the 1955 coup.

THE JEDDAH MILITARY PACT

When Gamal Abdul Nasser came to power in Egypt by eliminating one of the oldest monarchies in the Middle East, the Arab kings viewed the event with alarm. Their fear of the Egyptian Revolution heightened as Nasser's popularity and political strength both in Egypt and elsewhere increased. He became the rallying force for Arab awakening. Arab nationalism was resurrected, becoming the single most important concept in the Arab world.

Nasser's surprising political successes gained him the attention of many Arabs both in Egypt and in other Arab states. To many Arabs, he became a hero. Among those who took Nasser to their hearts was Mohammed al-Badr. Al-Badr had met Nasser in 1954 and was impressed. He believed that he shared similar political views with Nasser, and this influenced him to initiate a personal relationship with the Egyptian president. Such a relationship was based on the needs of Yemen and on the regional political strategy of President Nasser.

The close relationship between Nasser and al-Badr was strengthened after al-Badr became crown prince in 1955. Al-Badr was able to convince his father that close cooperation with Egypt was necessary to frustrate British imperialism in Aden and the protectorate. Thus, in early 1956, al-Badr was sent to Egypt and to the Soviet bloc countries in search of economic and military assistance. In the same year al-Badr was instrumental in influencing his father to join Egypt and Saudi Arabia in a mutual defense pact. In April 1956, Imam Ahmad left Yemen for the first time and went to Saudi Arabia to sign the Jeddah Military Pact with Saudi Arabia and Egypt. Among its 12 articles, Article Two is the most significant because it was later used by both Egypt and Saudi Arabia to legalize their intervention in Yemeni affairs. Article Two states:

> The contracting States consider any armed aggression committed against any State thereof or against their forces as an aggression against them. Therefore, and in implementation of the legitimate individual and collective right for the defence of their entity, each of them is bound to hasten to the assistance of the State against whom aggression is committed and to adopt forthwith all measures and to use all means at its disposal, including the use of its armed forces, in order to repel aggression and to restore security and peace.[7]

The Jeddah Military Pact afforded Yemen the opportunity to implement three objectives deemed essential by the imamate regime.

First, the pact was directly aimed at frustrating the British plan to federate the different principalities and sultanates comprising Aden and the protectorate. Initiated in 1952, the plan's objective was to intensify British control by increasing British personnel in the territory. In 1934, British interest in the protectorate was represented by two officials—a political officer and a political secretary. In the early 1950s, the number of British personnel present in the area increased by 3,000 percent[8] or by 6,000 people. Imam Ahmad viewed the British objective as a direct threat to Yemen's claim on the territory and as an endeavor to create a South Yemeni nationalism that would develop South Yemen as an entity apart from Yemen. Consequently, Yemen began frontier conflicts in 1954 and intensified the attacks in the latter part of that year. Yemen referred the dispute to the Arab League. The league was only able to assert its moral support for the legitimate Yemeni position over the question of the southern regions.[9] The incapacity of the Arab League to assist Yemen in its conflict with Great Britain induced the regime to seek help from other sources, notably from Egypt. Egypt, an opponent of imperialism, had recently extricated itself from the economic and political influence of the Western powers.

Second, the pact was aimed at offsetting the Turkish-Iraqi alliance promulgated in April 1955,[10] which became known as the Baghdad Pact. The Yemeni regime viewed the Turkish-Iraqi alliance as contrary to Arab interests, in particular to Yemeni interests, because Great Britain was associated with it. In fact, Britain became a primary member of the Baghdad Pact.

Finally, Yemen's alliance with revolutionary Egypt was aimed at placating reformist Yemenis as well as Arab nationalism. By associating itself with Egypt, Yemen became a proponent of Arab nationalism. It, moreover, reflected Yemen's tilt to the left on matters of foreign policy. Before 1956, Yemen abstained from voting in the United Nations on East-West issues. After 1956, Yemen followed Egypt's lead in voting against the West on Cold War problems.[11]

In the face of British intransigence, Yemen's isolationism progressively wore away. Similarly, Yemen's incoherence enlarged, and the thesis/antithesis conflict intensified. In order to restore a semblance of coherence, the regime aligned itself with Egypt. But the alliance, though essential in confirming Yemen's antiimperialism, was detrimental to the Yemeni traditional system because modern ideas were permitted further access into the country. Such a venture disturbed and alienated many Yemeni conservatives and ulema, who viewed the alliance as contrary to traditional values. The Free Yemenis and other reform-minded Yemenis welcomed the imam's regional association and considered it constructive.

The imam's regional and international associations began as early as 1951. In that year, Yemen established diplomatic relations with the United States and with Great Britain. Yemen's foreign policy tilt to the left began in 1955 when the imam, encouraged by his son, established diplomatic relations with the Soviet Union. In the following year, Yemen had diplomatic ties with Communist China and with most of the Eastern bloc nations. These diplomatic initiatives illustrated the change in the political attitude of the Yemeni government with respect to the escalation of the thesis/antithesis incoherence. It was apparent to the Yemeni regime that international involvements were the source of modern ideas. But political circumstances prevailed, and Yemen was motivated to establish regional and international associations.

It was natural that the establishment of diplomatic relations with the Eastern bloc countries would be followed by arrangements for large shipments of arms to Yemen. By 1957, Yemen was thriving with Egyptian and Soviet army personnel and instructors. The increase of foreign personnel intensified the friction between traditionalists and reformists. But incoherence was relatively controlled by Yemen's association with revolutionary Egypt and by its foreign policy position.

CONFEDERATION WITH THE UNITED ARAB
REPUBLIC

The close cooperation between Yemen and Egypt after the Jeddah Pact led to the formation of a confederation between Yemen and the United Arab Republic on March 8, 1958. The United Arab Republic had been formed the previous month between Egypt and Syria, a crowning achievement for President Nasser. The unity between Yemen and the U.A.R. formed the United Arab States.

The United Arab States Pact created the formation of a supreme council, composed of the heads of the member states; a defense council; an economic council; and a cultural council. The pact maintained that each state "will preserve its international personality and its system of government."[12]

Imam Ahmad's unexpected move to join the United Arab States was a move of political sophistication on the one hand and a political blunder on the other. It caused regional and international responses.

Regionally, the imam gained Nasser's support for his struggle with Britain over Aden and the protectorate. It also silenced the "Voice of the Arabs" and conciliated the Free Yemenis outside of Yemen. However, the imam was obliged to permit more foreign personnel to come into Yemen. This was what Ahmad did not want, since more foreign contingents in Yemen implied an increase in foreign ideas and an intensification in incoherence. Nonetheless, the confederation was helpful in saving Yemen's fragile system when the intra-Arab power struggle became dangerous to the Arab conservative regimes in 1958. Nasser's political objective in his power struggle with the conservative regimes of Saudi Arabia, Jordan, and Iraq became direct. His motives were to eliminate anachronistic Arab regimes that were closely associated with the Western powers and to replace them with nationalistic governments anxious to create Arab unity.[13] Thus, a republic was created out of the ruins of the old regime of King Faisal and Nuri Said in Iraq; President Shamoun of Lebanon was literally forced to resign, and only the landing of U.S. Marines saved the country from a bloody civil war; King Hussein of Jordan was saved by the landing of British paratroopers; and King Saud of Saudi Arabia was dodging attempts on his life. It seemed that by July of 1958, the old order was to be swept aside in one major wave of militant pan-Arabism.[14] The Arab power struggle became international when the Western and Eastern blocs took particular interest in the intra-Arab rivalry. The West, anxious to preserve the conservative Arab regimes in order to maintain and to promote its economic interests in the region, opted to extend its support to those governments. The status quo was to be preserved. When the Western powers had thus committed themselves, the revolutionary Arab regimes turned to the Soviet Union for support. "With such augmented strength, these nationalists wished first to break the Western monopoly of influence and prerogative in the area, and then free themselves from dependence on any single great power."[15]

Internationally, Yemen gained the praise of the Soviet Union for confederating with the U.A.R.[16] The imam became the recipient of high praise from the Soviet bloc. The Soviets had always criticized Yemen's antiquated social and political organizations. But after the Soviet-Yemeni treaty of 1955, they became more tolerant toward Yemen, and Soviet historians lauded Yemeni and southern Arabian resistance to British imperialism.[17] The Soviets endorsed Yemen's border conflict with Britain and urged other Arab states to lend their support to it so that the federation of the protectorate would fail. Nevertheless, the Soviets criticized the imam's unresponsiveness to changing the backwardness of his people, blaming Western imperialism rather than the social, political, and economic infrastructure in Yemen.

The Soviet attitude toward Yemen fluctuated from criticism to tolerance, depending on the state of their relationship at a particular moment. Prior to 1955, Soviet criticism and castigation of Imam Ahmad was virulent. However, when Yemen improved its relations with Egypt and with the Soviet Union, Soviet criticism of the imam ceased. The blame for Yemen's backwardness was no longer placed on the shoulders of the royal family, but on Western, particularly British, imperialism. The improved relationship between Yemen and the Soviet Union won the imam Soviet commendation for his attempts to improve the health, education, and economic conditions of his people.[18] In fact, the imam was considered by the Soviets as a progressive and enlightened leader. Relations between Yemen and the Soviet Union reached an all-time high when the imam agreed to permit the Soviets to construct the port of Hodeida and to accept Soviet economic, technical, and medical assistance.

U.S. response to Yemen's confederation with the United Arab Republic was rather indifferent. The U.S. government viewed the events in the Middle East with a certain degree of consternation. Its indifference was a reflection of the cool relations between the United States and the Yemeni government. The Yemeni regime believed that the United States was inextricably tied to British imperialism in Aden and that the U.S. government was the most important major power defending the state of Israel. On a personal note, the imam believed that the U.S. government was supporting his brother, al-Hassan, in opposition to his son.[19] However, the U.S. attitude toward Yemen was influenced by the antagonism of al-Badr. Al-Badr stood in front of the Americans as an avowed hostile opponent.[20] Consequently, the U.S. government saw no need to officially comment on political developments in Yemen.

The ramifications of the confederation on Yemen were felt during the regency of al-Badr. In April of 1959, Imam Ahmad went to Italy for medical treatment, delegating his son as regent during his absence.

Under the regency of al-Badr, Yemen became embroiled in chaos and confusion. Al-Badr placed Egyptian personnel in such key positions as the Directorate of Security and replaced the governor of Taiz. These actions were aimed at reforming the administration of the government. His attempts at reform increased Zeidi criticism of him and, once again, raised the issue of his competency. In the meantime, the army in Sanaa, burdened by the lack of decent living accommodations, rioted.

This was followed by demands for more pay. Al-Badr promised to increase its pay by 25 percent. Army disturbances also occurred in Taiz, where the governor of the city was dragged from his home and placed under arrest. The tribes of the Hashid and Bakil were once more summoned to the aid of the ruling family. However, al-Badr had to bribe them to acquire their support. This measure depleted the state's treasury.

Al-Badr was not able to keep his promise to the army, and the tribes became well aware of his inability to be authoritative. His reform measures alienated the Zeidis, who were the primary victims of his reform movement, and the army, which was the recipient of broken promises. [21]

In his attempt to reform the administration of the government, al-Badr lost Zeidi support as well as the backing of the Free Yemenis. His attempts reinforced the opinion held by many Yemenis that "al-Badr was well-meaning but wholly a nonentity who could not possibly replace the authority of his father." [22]

Imam Ahmad returned to Yemen and immediately reinstated order. He punished the primary insurrectionists. He also executed the leading chief of the Hashid tribe and the chief's son, alleged to have conspired to overthrow the imamate and institute a republic.

Although the imam was able to reestablish order, incoherence had already progressed during his absence. The fact that al-Badr could not use the value of emanation to stabilize the situation indicated the withering away of that element in the Yemeni society. By removing Zeidis from positions of authority, he inadvertently increased the friction between the reformists and the traditionalists. Imam Ahmad's execution of the leading chief of the Hashid tribe and of the chief's son meant a valuable loss of tribal support for the ruling family and, therefore, a loss for traditionalism. Moreover, it implied an erosion of the imam's ability to serve as the final arbiter in tribal discord. It also impaired his capacity to insist on direct bargaining, between himself and the tribes or among the tribes. In direct bargaining, "individuals and groups make demands on each other and negotiate directly with each other." [23] The breakdown of direct bargaining along with emanation affected the imamate structure's ability to survive. The imam's aura was fading, and his ability to use subjection was soon to deteriorate because changes were being demanded from the lower echelon of the Yemeni society. "As long as change takes place solely at the command of the more powerful polar occupant, continuity remains assured." [24]

THE DISMEMBERMENT OF THE CONFEDERATION

The end of the confederation between Yemen and the United Arab Republic began after the return of Imam Ahmad from Italy. His cruel method of suppressing the insurrection proved to the Free Yemenis that he must be removed from the imamate. It was during this time that the Free Yemenis altered their political aim. While they had previously worked to eliminate the Hamid al-Din rule, not the imamate itself, now they began to work toward the overthrow of the imamate institution and toward the establishment of a republic.[25] It was also during this time that Nasser chose the Free Yemenis as his instrument for the elimination of the imamate and as the means toward the expansion of his political influence in the Arabian Peninsula.[26] Egypt's intention in Yemen became evident after Syria seceded from the United Arab Republic in September 1961. A document was captured from Lieutenant-Colonel Ali Fahmy, who had established an espionage cell in Sanaa. The document, seized by the Syrian Public Security Police in Aleppo, asserted:

The union of the Yemen with the U.A.R. will not liberate the Yemeni people from the Imamic regime unless the throne itself is destroyed as Farouk's throne was overturned and replaced by a republic.

As long as the Imamic regime continues to function we shall not be able to impose the same system that we have introduced into Syria which by virtue of its union with Egypt has become part of our nation. It should take little effort to control the course of events in Syria and to retain our authority over it.

On the other hand, the Zeidi rite, to which the majority of the Yemeni belong, stands as a stumbling block in the way of the establishment of the Socialistic order which constitutes the foundation of the new era that we have brought into being . . .

The best tactic that we can adopt to win over the Yemeni to our program is to effectuate a coup d'etat. This can be executed successfully through bribing Yemeni army officers who are close to the Imam and who command his confidence.[27]

Such a plan, however, could not be implemented while Yemen was still officially confederated with the United Arab Republic. This obstacle was soon to be eliminated.

The imam had shown an attitude hostile to Nasser's socialistic principles. Socialism, as adopted in Egypt, gave rise to a
submerged discord between Yemen and Egypt. The imam kept
silent until after Syria seceded from the U.A.R. Encouraged by
the secession of Syria, Imam Ahmad let his philosophical opposition to socialism surface. He wrote a poem criticizing socialism
and those who nationalize the property of the people and who
permit what Islam had prohibited.[28] The poem was broadcast
on Radio Sanaa and published in Yemeni newspapers. It in-
directly attacked Nasser's socialistic practices.

The imam's poem sparked the anger of Nasser, who terminated the confederation on December 27, 1961. The Egyptian
government, on the same day, declared on Cairo radio that
there was nothing to be found in the nature of the two governments that could promote a federation. It stated that the confederation could not erect sound policies to alleviate the problems
of social development and that the experience of the past three
years proved that the Yemeni people did not profit from the
experience of the confederation.[29]

About two weeks after the termination of the confederation,
the "Voice of the Arabs" was urging the Yemenis to revolt against
the imam, identifying him with imperialism. Moreover, the Free
Yemenis in Cairo were permitted to begin their active agitation
for change in Yemen. Cairo radio described Mohammed Zubeiri
as the leader of the Yemeni Liberation Movement in Cairo and
Abdul Rahman Beidhani as the chief representative of the revolutionary movement. On January 22, 1962, Beidhani was introduced
in Rose el-Youssef.

Most of the leaders of the Free Yemenis were former friends
and confidants of al-Badr. Al-Badr had also befriended Abdullah
Sallal, who was jailed by Imam Ahmad for his role in the 1948
coup. Al-Badr not only urged Sallal's release, but also thought
him to be a well-meaning reformist and a liberal thinker.[30]
Sallal was given the post of harbor master at Hodeida by al-
Badr. In 1959, Sallal came into contact with Egyptians. It was
surmised that it was during this year that the Egyptians selected
him to lead the future coup against the imamic regime.[31] During
Sallal's tenure as harbor master at Hodeida, the imam had been
shot several times at the Hodeida hospital after having had an
X-ray examination. Sallal was released from his job by the imam
because the imam suspected him of having a role in the attempted
assassination. Al-Badr immediately made Sallal the chief of his
personal guards, without the imam's objections.[32] Al-Badr's
confidence in those whom he believed shared his political thinking
was unlimited. "The confidence he placed in his supposed friends

in fact admitted the Nasserites to the most sensitive inner structure of Imamic power and prepared its destruction."[33] Al-Badr also had a keen trust in President Nasser. On November 11, 1962, al-Badr lamented after he had been deposed: "I always considered him (Nasser) as a friend and a brother and believed in his promises."[34]

The radio propaganda campaign from Cairo proved effective in increasing tension and disorder in Yemen. Disturbances occurred in Sanaa and Taiz. The imam responded by appealing to the people to respect the principles of Islam and to cease from rioting and disturbing the peace. However, demonstrations continued unabated through the remainder of the imam's life.

In the last year of Imam Ahmad's reign, incoherence had increased dramatically. The imam's illness after 1959 reduced his capacity to take charge of his governmental duties as he had done before. After the attempt on his life, he became less able to carry the burdens of administering the government. He was, therefore, forced to delegate political authority to al-Badr, who managed to intensify the incoherence by being too receptive to the reformists. The growth of incoherence was manifestly apparent during the riots that occurred after the dismemberment of the confederation. The fact that the people did not heed the imam's appeal to restore order and tranquility indicated that the values of emanation and subjection as stabilizing elements had become mute. The antithesis had changed the attitude of a great many Yemenis. Thus, only one week after the death of Imam Ahmad on September 18, 1962, the revolution erupted. The imamate was destroyed, and the Sayyid power was eliminated.

NOTES

1. The use of Halpern's theory on incoherence was used by Kathryn Boals in her Ph.D. dissertation, Modernization and Intervention: Yemen as a Theoretical Case Study (Princeton University, 1970).

2. Manfred Halpern, "A redefinition of the Revolutionary Situation," Journal of International Affairs 23 (1969):55.

3. Ibid., p. 58.

4. Halpern's polarities of encounter are incoherence, emanation, subjection, isolation, buffering, direct bargaining, boundary management, and transformation.

5. Ibid., p. 63.

6. Ibid., p. 61.

7. Muhammed Khalil, The Arab States and the Arab League: A Documentary Record, vol. 2 (Beirute: Khayats, 1962), p. 251.

8. Bernard Reilly, Aden and the Yemen (London: Her Majesty's Stationary Office, 1960), pp. 461-63.

9. Ibid., p. 180.

10. Sir Kennedy Trevaskis, Shades of Amber (London: Hutchinson, 1968), p. 93.

11. GAOR, 5th-19th sess., plen. mtgs. (1950-62).

12. Khalil, The Arab States and the Arab League, p. 643.

13. George Lenczowski, "The Objects and Methods of Nasserism," Journal of International Affairs 19 (November 1965): 67.

14. Ibid.

15. Manfred Halpern, The Politics of Social Change in the Middle East and North Africa (Princeton: Princeton University Press, 1963), p. 371.

16. Stephen Page, USSR and Arabia (London: Central Asian Research Center, 1971), p. 48.

17. Ivo J. Lederer and Wayne Vucinich, eds., The Soviet Union and the Middle East (Stanford: Stanford University Press, 1974), p. 214.

18. Ibid.

19. Zaid al-Wazir, Muhawalt li-Fahm al-Mashkelah al-Yamaniah ("An Attempt to Understand the Yemeni Problem") (Beirute: al-Sharikah al-Muttahedah lil-Towze'e, 1968), p. 197.

20. Ibid., p. 188.

21. For more details on al-Badr's regency see Harold Ingrams, The Yemen: Imams, Rulers, and Revolution (London: 1963), pp. 109-10.

22. Dana A. Schmidt, Yemen: The Unknown War (New York: Holt, Rinehart & Winston, 1968), p. 44.

23. Halpern, "A Redefinition of the Revolutionary Situation," pp. 63-64.

24. Ibid., p. 62.

25. George Haddad, Revolution and Military Rule in the Middle East (Santa Barbara: University of California Press, 1973), p. 240.

26. Ibid., pp. 240-41.

27. Stanko Guldescu, "The Background of the Yemeni Revolution of 1962," Dalhousie Review 45 (Spring 1965):68-69.

28. The full text of the imam's poem can be found in Salah al-Din al-Munjad, al-Yaman wa al-Muttahedah bain al-Ittihad wa al-Infisal ("Yemen and the United Arab Republic between Unity and Disunity") (Beirute: Daar al-Kitab al-Jadid, 1962), pp. 37-41.

29. The text of the Cairo broadcast can be found in Ibid., pp. 42-44.

30. Schmidt, Yemen: The Unknown War, p. 71.

31. Haddad, Revolution and Military Rule in the Middle East, p. 242.

32. Schmidt, Yemen: The Unknown War, p. 73.

33. Ibid.

34. Spiro Elis, "Dead King Has Plan to Return to Palace," Washington Post, November 11, 1962, p. A-20.

PART III
Era of
Civil War

5

IMPACT OF THE 1962 YEMENI REVOLUTION

Mohammed al-Badr became the imam of Yemen immediately after his father's death. However, al-Badr's friendship with Nasser was not helpful in restraining the "Voice of the Arabs" from personally attacking him. Cairo radio referred to him as the "new tyrant," and the Free Yemenis were allowed by the Egyptian authorities to call for his overthrow. It seemed that Nasser had decided not to allow al-Badr to rule Yemen and to try to develop the Yemeni society economically and industrially.[1]

On September 26, 1962, revolutionary tanks in Sanaa opened fire on al-Badr's palace. The revolutionaries seized Radio Sanaa and proclaimed a republic. Led by Abdullah Sallal,[2] the insurgents began to systematically liquidate the ruling elements of the old regime, in particular the Sayyids.[3] The revolutionaries also confiscated the property of the leaders of the old regime. Members of the old order outside of the kingdom were tried in absentia, and their citizenship was revoked.

The coup immediately instituted the Revolutionary Command Council (RCC) and the Presidential Council. The former was made up of eight members and headed by Sallal.[4] The latter was composed of three members. The RCC then issued its objectives, which were divided into three categories: the internal stage, the Arab nationalist stage, and the international stage. In general, the objectives called for the reinstitution of the Shari'a as the law of the land, the construction of social justice through a social system wholly in agreement with the Shari'a, the initiation of a cultural and educational revolution that would quicken the elimination of illiteracy and ignorance, the belief in Arab nationalism and Arab unity, the commitment to nonalign-

ment, the association of the revolutionary regime with other
Arab revolutionary states, and the enhancement of resistance
to imperialism.[5]

> The Yemeni coup was thus followed by the standard
> type of political and social changes that had become
> a common pattern in the Arab revolutionary move-
> ments: the establishment of a republic, the removal
> of the old ruling class, the end of big landlordism,
> the creation of a public sector, and the transition
> towards a socialist economy. Old, backward, and
> isolated Yemen was thus suddenly omitted from the
> list of reactionary states and was reclassified among
> the "liberated" Arab states who, moreover, were
> expected to follow a policy of non-alignment accom-
> panied by cooperation with "the friendly nations"
> (i.e., those of the Communist Bloc), and must raise
> the banner of struggle against the "old and new
> imperialism" in order to qualify for the title.[6]

This chapter examines the involvement of Egypt and Saudi
Arabia in Yemeni affairs and the attitude of other Arab states
toward the conflict. It also evaluates the roles of the United
States and the United Nations in their attempts to resolve the
Yemeni war. Finally, this chapter studies the effect of the
conflict on Yemeni society. However, it is essential to pause
temporarily in order to examine the concepts of influence, involvement, and intervention. This endeavor is necessary because
the analysis refers to both Egyptian and Saudi roles in Yemeni
affairs as intervention. A conceptual understanding of the
terms is, therefore, imperative in order to fully comprehend
the roles of Egypt, Saudi Arabia, and other parties in the
affairs of Yemen.

The concepts of influence, involvement, and intervention
are defined by Howard Wriggins in his article, "Political Outcomes of Foreign Assistance: Influence, Involvement, and Intervention."[7] To Wriggins, influence carries a benign connotation
in international affairs. States have been peacefully influencing
each other for centuries. Diplomats attempt to persuade their
counterparts to look at a problem or interest in much the same
way as they do.[8]

> However, it is obvious that in any particular diplo-
> matic transaction a diplomat's "persuasiveness" will
> depend in part upon the power relations obtained

between the two, and with power relations in the
equation a certain degree of intimidation may be
implicit. Thus, even "influence" as between two
diplomats may be derived from implicit political pressure, and not be simply the outcome of one man's
ability to marshal arguments or evoke friendly feelings on the part of the man to be influenced . . .
It (influence) does not imply actions within another
state's territory, except those normal in traditional
diplomatic exchanges. [9]

As to involvement, Wriggins emphasizes that "it implies
close cooperation or 'mutual involvement,' as two or more states
work toward agreed and often shared purposes."[10] In involvement there are shared ends and the means are usually acceptable
on a mutual basis.

Intervention, unlike involvement and influence, is the
extreme end of the spectrum. It is the stage that:

. . . connotes action in another's territory, but
where purposes diverge and a threat is implicit.
Two states are involved, but not in mutually acceptable activities. Intervention may be characterized
as an effort 1) to manipulate the internal affairs of
foreign policy activities of another state; and 2)
generally accompanied by the threat of hostile
action.[11]

Wriggins adds:

"Intervention" may be distinguished from other
types of influence by the simple criteria of whether
the regime or the opposition groups, respectively,
favor or disapprove of what is being done. What
is assistance to one observer may appear as intervention to another.[12]

Professor Charles O. Lerche, Jr. defines intervention as
"the interference by one state in the internal affairs of another,
and may assume either defensive or offensive forms."[13] Defensive intervention aims at preserving a particular regime or system,
and offensive intervention attempts to alter such a system. The
former aims at preserving the balance of power in a particular
area, while the latter desires to materially change the balance
of power in its favor. The purpose of offensive intervention
is to cause a government or a policy in another state to change.[14]

REGIONAL IMPACT

The Yemeni Revolution was potentially dangerous to peace in the Middle East. A regional response to the revolution came immediately from Egypt and Saudi Arabia and later from other Arab states.

Egyptian Response

Twenty-four hours after the Yemeni Revolution was announced, an Egyptian expeditionary force arrived in Yemen via the newly finished port of Hodeida. Soon after the revolution was proclaimed, resistance from the northern highland Zeidi tribes formed under the leadership of Prince al-Hassan, who had arrived in Yemen via Saudi Arabia from New York. To counter the Egyptian involvement in Yemen, Saudi Arabia aided the royalists in their attempts to return to power.

The Egyptian presence in Yemen catalyzed a local dispute between the Yemeni traditionalists and the Yemeni reformists into an armed confrontation. The Yemeni revolutionaries would probably not have attempted to alter the political, economic, and social structure of Yemen had they not been sure of active Egyptian support. They knew that imamic rule, with all its faults, was still predominantly accepted by the Yemenis. Moreover, they knew that the foundations of imamic rule were correct and positive in that the foundations permitted and encouraged the development of physical as well as mental human aspects. However, because the imams tended to violate the precepts of imamic rule, the imamate became associated with stagnation, corruption, and dishonesty.

Active Egyptian support of the revolution was imperative if success were to be realized by the Yemeni revolutionaries. Mohammed al-Attar in his book, al-Takhaluf al-Igtisadi wa al-Ijtima'i fi al-Yaman ("The Economic and Social Backwardness in Yemen"), notes that without active Egyptian support, the Yemeni revolutionaries would have faced far greater difficulties.[15] Ahmad Sharaf al-Din in his book, al-Yaman abr al-Ta'rikh ("Yemen in History"), asserts that the difference between the revolution of September 1962 and previous coups in Yemen was that the latter were without outside support. Consequently, no sooner had they started than they were quelled.[16] Nonetheless, Egyptian and Saudi involvement in Yemen enlarged the conflict from a local struggle to a regional dilemma.

Instead of being restricted to a local struggle between
royalists and republicans, or conservatives and
reformists, or moderate reformists and social revolutionaries, the Yemeni civil war thus became an international military and ideological conflict in which the
Egyptian military effort on the republican side was
approved by the radical socialist Arab regimes with
the Soviet Bloc and China, while the Saudi aid in
funds and arms to the royalists was supported and
approved by the Arab monarchies and certain Western
powers. [17]

Nasser's immediate dispatch of an expeditionary force into
Yemen to help the republicans may be attributed to several
factors. First, the National Charter, inaugurated in May of
1962 by Nasser, establishing an ideological basis for socialism
in Egypt, declared:

Revolution is the only means by which the Arab Nation
can free itself of its shackles, and rid itself of the
dark heritage which burdened it. For, the elements
of suppression and exploitation which long dominated
the Arab Nation and seized its wealth will never will-
ingly submit. [18]

Moreover, the Charter asserted:

The United Arab Republic, firmly convinced that
she is an integral part of the Arab Nation, must
propagate her call for unity and the principles it
embodies, so that it would be at the disposal of
every Arab citizen, without hesitating for one minute
before the outworn argument that this would be considered an interference in the affairs of others. [19]

Second, "elements of traditionalism and reaction against foreign
influence are present but Arabism is characteristically the feeling
that the only way for the Arabs to be anything is for them to
be themselves." [20] Third,

President Nasser seized on the revolution in Yemen
in September, 1962 as an opportunity to break out
of his isolation in the wake of Syria's secession from
the United Arab Republic, and regain the initiative
in Arab affairs for Egypt on the basis of revolutionary leadership. [21]

Fourth, it suggests:

> . . . the Egyptians were caught up in their own
> rhetoric to the point that they actually believed
> that what was hindering the achievement of Arab
> unity on the basis of revolutionary socialism was
> a small group of reactionary leaders and that the
> Arab "masses" were in fact ready to fall behind
> Egyptian leadership in sweeping away the few re-
> actionary obstacles to the fulfillment of their common
> dream. [22]

Fifth, Egyptian action in Yemen was viewed as a continuation
of Egyptian desire to strengthen its influence in the Arabian
Peninsula and, by so doing, to deny Western imperialism the
opportunity to continue its presence in the Arab world. Finally,
the official explanation given by Egypt for its military involvement in Yemen was that Sallal had asked for help in protecting
the new regime from its enemies. [23]

Egyptian intervention in Yemeni affairs was an error not
realized by the Egyptian authorities until 1965. By that time,
they were too embroiled in the conflict, which had become a
matter of national honor. They were frustrated, having assumed
that royalist resistance would wither away on their arrival.
When resistance did not cease, Egypt increased its expeditionary
force from a reported 13,000 in December 1962 to an estimated
70,000 by December 1966. Moreover, the Egyptians became
involved in the daily affairs of the Yemeni people without a
theoretical conception of the nature of the Yemeni society. As
such, they alienated many republicans, who spoke openly of
Egyptian imperialism and Egyptian heavy-handedness. One
such blunder was the creation of a highly centralized, Egyptian-
style administrative bureaucracy in which no allowances for
local autonomy or decentralized decision making were made. [24]
Furthermore, the Egyptians shoveled republican regimes at will.
This added to the political and social fragmentation already
apparent in the Yemeni society and increased the cleavages
among republican ranks. Such methods gave rise to an independent party under Ibrahim al-Wazir, nephew of Abdullah al-
Wazir, called the Yemeni Popular Forces Union (YPFU), which
came to be known as the "Third Force." The YPFU raised the
issue of foreign domination and demanded the termination of
all Egyptian and Saudi intervention. Furthermore, it called
for the restoration of the Shari'a and the implementation of
shura (consultation). The YPFU viewed both the royalists and

the republicans as violators of Islamic law. It demanded an end to the fighting and the creation of machineries that would generate a public response to the future political system in Yemen.[25] Because of Egyptian conceptual unpreparedness, the Egyptians were unable to defeat the royalists or to maintain harmony within republican ranks.

Egyptian heavy-handedness was felt by tribes, who had originally been neutral in the conflict. By treating neutralists as enemies, the Egyptians inadvertently alienated many Yemenis, who consequently flocked to the royalist side. Moreover, the Egyptians conceptualized the war in Yemen as a military conflict between two organized groups. Their method was to strike at the royalists by conventional military means. Thus, the bombing of villages and straffing of farming areas under royalist control was common. This military venture was primarily aimed at convincing the people to abandon support for the royalists. However, it only intensified hatred of the Egyptian authorities. Moreover, such a method alienated even republican regions, because needed social changes were neglected in favor of military strategy. "What the Egyptians failed to realize was that the basic struggle was not against the Royalists as an organized, structured opponent, but rather against the forces of fragmentation and cleavage inherent in the structure of Yemeni society."[26] Hence, they failed.

In sum, the Egyptian role in Yemen was intervention. They not only had a military presence in Yemen, but Egyptians were also involved in the policymaking of the republican regime. In fact, they were the administrators, executors, and implementors of military and political policies. Their active and personal attention helped to preserve the republican regime. Their heavy-handed methods attest not only to their attempts to manipulate and control the foreign policy of Yemen, but also to their lack of understanding of the Yemeni society.

Saudi Arabian Response

The Saudi Arabian role in the Yemeni conflict came as a result of the establishment of a republican regime in Yemen and as a consequence of Egyptian intervention. Saudi involvement was essentially defensive and conservative.[27] It feared the establishment of a republican regime in Yemen because of its potential danger to the Saudi regime, which, according to Kathryn Boals, was as vulnerable to the onslaught of certain "modern ideas" as Yemen had been during the 1930s.[28] Thus,

King Saud began arming the royalists in an attempt to stymie
the Egyptian presence in Yemen and to keep the republicans
occupied with an internal war and away from Saudi territory.
As a result of Saudi involvement in Yemen, two Saudi pilots
defected to Egypt with their planes, and Egyptian forces were
subsequently increased in Yemen.[29] Saudi Arabian forces were
incapable of defending Saudi territory against Egyptian incursions that occurred several times during the latter part of 1962
and early in 1963. Thus, the Saudi government adopted a three-
pronged policy intended to ensure its security from the potentially
dangerous events in Yemen: to have the United States formally
declare its support of Saudi integrity, to develop the capability
of the Yemeni royalist forces so that the royalists would be able
to keep both United Arab Republic (U.A.R.) and Yemen Arab
Republic forces engaged in Yemen and away from Saudi territory,
and to remove the threat of U.A.R. forces from the Arabian
Peninsula. The interests of the royalists were consistently
subordinated to the third objective.[30]

Saudi determination to remove the Egyptians from Yemen
intensified after Faisal succeeded his brother, Saud, in November
of 1964. Massive doses of money and arms were supplied to the
royalists. But the supplies tended to slacken whenever Saudi
Arabia believed it necessary to give the U.A.R. a chance to
extricate itself from Yemen. This occurred after agreements
were reached between Egypt and Saudi Arabia, aimed at ending
their respective interventions.

When Saudi Arabia saw the inevitability of Egyptian withdrawal from Yemen, it changed its political objective regarding
the Yemeni republic. Previously, Saudi Arabia had worked to
bring an end to the republic because it symbolized the new
ideology—modernity, Arab unity, and social progress. However,
when it became evident that the republic had no formulated
ideology, Saudi objectives were altered. In 1969, its opposition
to the republic was shelved in favor of sustaining a weak republican regime in Sanaa. Such a policy aimed at fostering the
historical animosity between the tribes and the central government by carefully keeping the two parties equal in strength.
Saudi funds were made available to both the republican government and to the tribes. Each faction, therefore, became dependent upon Saudi money for its existence.

This Saudi policy only intensifies incoherence in the Yemeni
society. Its submergence is temporary because the element of
incoherence may erupt into violence. Such an eruption may
not be caused by internal forces in Yemen; rather it may come
from the outside, presumably from the People's Democratic

Republic of South Yemen, whose political philosophy and objectives are contradictory to those of Saudi Arabia. The potential danger to the Saudi government would be overwhelming, since a regional conflict could endanger the longevity of traditionalist Saudi Arabia.

Saudi involvement in Yemen was an attempt to reinstate the ancien régime by massive doses of financial and military assistance. As such, the Saudi role must be considered as intervention. It is true that the Saudi government did not send military personnel into Yemen, but it did allow the royalists to use its territory as a sanctuary. Saudi help to the royalists was undertaken not only to influence political and military events in Yemen, but also to give the royalists credence in international affairs. But when the royalist cause became less credible, the Saudis shelved their commitment to the royalists for the sake of political rapprochement with the republican regime in Sanaa.

Intra-Arab Response

Intra-Arab response to the Yemeni conflict was as varied as were the Arab states in their ideological beliefs. There were the radical, socialist regimes of Egypt, Iraq, Syria, and Algeria; the moderate republics of Lebanon, Sudan, and Tunisia; and the conservative monarchies of Saudi Arabia, Jordan, and Libya. The socialist regimes tended, in general, to support the republican government in Sanaa, giving it quick recognition. They also gave it their unreserved support, with the exception of Syria. The moderate Arab republics were, on the whole, not enthusiastic about the revolutionary regime in Yemen, but they gave it quick recognition. They believed that the revolutionary Yemenis were radical in their politics and highly vengeful in their actions. The conservative monarchies opposed the overthrow of the imamate, in particular Saudi Arabia and Jordan. The revolutionary, socialist regimes were outspoken in their demands and tended to speak on "behalf of the Arabs." Consequently, the nonsocialist, nonrevolutionary Arab governments were forced into silence.

The Arab states, with the exception of Saudi Arabia and Jordan, remained aloof and watched Arab blood being wasted by Arabs.

Even the ultra-Arab nationalists of the Ba'ath ruling party in Syria never denounced Nasser for keeping his forces in Yemen and killing fellow Arabs. For

> them and for other revolutionaries, Arab socialism
> and revolution took precedence over Arab national-
> ism.[31]

There were, however, a few voices raised among the intellectual
elite in the Arab world admonishing Nasser's involvement in
Yemen. These voices contended that Nasser was forsaking the
struggle against Israel for the sake of sustaining a corrupt,
inefficient regime in Sanaa. Even when Egypt was alleged and
later substantiated to have used poison gas on Yemeni villages
in royalist areas, Arab criticism of Nasser's action remained
relatively the same.[32]

ROLE OF THE UNITED STATES

The Yemeni dilemma came at a time when the United States
was involved crucially in the Cuban missile crisis of 1962.
Yemen was very far from its mind. Nonetheless, the Kennedy
administration, as early as 1961, was reviewing its Middle Eastern policy. It also was studying ways to alter world opinion
that negatively associated it with supporting "reactionary"
regimes. In the case of Yemen, the United States could not
immediately give the republican regime recognition because of
the complexity of the situation. The Kennedy administration
could not overlook the fact that its friends, namely Saudi Arabia
and Jordan, were supporting Imam al-Badr. Moreover, Great
Britain, an ally of the United States, had withheld recognition
of the Yemeni republic and had voiced misgivings concerning
Egyptian intervention in Yemen. But the U.S. government
witnessed the quick recognition of the Yemeni republic by most
of the Arab states and by all of the Communist bloc, including
Communist China. The United States did not wish to remain
aloof from the Yemeni situation nor to allow the Communist states
free and unhindered influence in Yemen. It was largely due
to this latter factor that President Kennedy began to send
personal messages to Nasser and Faisal urging the two leaders
to subdue the situation.

Almost immediately after the revolution in Yemen was proclaimed, the Kennedy administration sent a letter to Prince
Faisal assuring the Saudi government of U.S. support. The
letter was not forwarded to Faisal until after the Saudi towns
of Najran and Jaizan had been bombarded by U.A.R. forces
in retaliation for Saudi support of the royalists. According to
the Egyptians, Saudi towns close to the Yemeni-Saudi border

were serving as a refuge for the royalists. Kennedy's letter was not made public until January 1963, after further Egyptian air raids on Saudi territory. The letter was meant to allay Saudi fears and to emphasize to the U.A.R. the U.S. obligation to preserve Saudi sovereignty. In the letter, President Kennedy said, "You may be assured of full U.S. support for the maintenance of Saudi Arabia integrity."[33]

While President Kennedy was keeping in touch with both Nasser and Faisal, the State Department contacted all those concerned with the Yemeni problem, except the imam.[34] The objective of the State Department was a settlement of the Yemeni conflict. Kennedy, at the end of November 1962, proposed steps toward a settlement to Crown Prince Faisal, King Hussein, and President Nasser. Once again, the imam, although still recognized officially by the United States, was left out.[35] The proposal called on Saudi Arabia to withhold further material aid to the royalists and asked the United Arab Republic to withdraw its forces from the country. The United States, fearing Egyptian rejection of its proposal, offered to recognize the republican regime in Yemen. On December 19, 1962, the U.S. government gave the Yemen Arab Republic full recognition. It had taken the United States three months to reach that decision. Recognition of the Yemeni republic was a policy also aimed at denying "the area of Soviet control" and permitting the United States to "remain on talking terms with all parties to the dispute."[36]

It became evident to the U.S. government that the Soviet Union, which in the last year of Imam Ahmad's reign was lurking in the wings and waiting for an opportunity to develop an effective position of influence in Yemen, had seized the Yemen Revolution as the opportunity to promote its political and economic influence. Accordingly, the Soviets lent full support to the new republic—arms, training, and economic assistance. The Soviet Union also swung the satellites under its influence quickly in line on behalf of the Yemen republic. The U.S. government apparently felt that U.S. recognition would also protect any U.S. interests in the area. In fact, the Kennedy administration hoped that U.S. recognition of the Yemeni republic would lessen the tensions between Egypt and Saudi Arabia and curtail Communist advances in the area.

U.S. recognition of the Sallal regime was granted after the Yemen republic promised to honor its international obligations, including the Treaty of Sanaa with Britain. The four-paragraph statement of recognition also mentioned U.A.R. willingness to "undertake a reciprocal disengagement and expeditious phased

removal of troops from Yemen as external forces engaged in
support of the Yemen royalists are removed from the frontier,
and as external support of the royalists is stopped."[37]

Recognition by the United States of the Yemeni regime in
Sanaa had mixed reactions. The Egyptians interpreted U.S.
recognition as a vindication of the coup that ousted the imam
and as evidence of U.S. good intentions in desiring to reevaluate
its Middle East policies. Anti-Nasser forces, both monarchists
and radical leftists in the Arab world, asserted that U.S. recognition of the Sallal regime proved that the United States was
committed to supporting Nasser.[38] This was what they had
alleged for months. They also emphasized that Egypt had promised to tone down its propaganda against Israel. Other Arab
elements contended that U.S. recognition was aimed at forestall-
ing a true settlement of the conflict, thereby keeping the Egyptian army occupied in Arabia and away from the borders of
Israel. But it seemed that:

> . . . among diplomats tuned into Washington, the
> explanation was that, after a long wrangle inside
> the State Department over recognition, the day was
> carried by the "New Frontier" element, who were
> anxious to prove that the U.S. is not necessarily
> committed to reactionary anachronistic regimes and
> is, on the contrary, anxious to help progressive
> young elements who are the wave of the future.[39]

Nevertheless, U.S. friends in the Arab world were stunned by
the U.S. recognition. King Hussein of Jordan declared that
"the United States was undercutting her friends and encouraging
the subversion of other legal governments and intervention in
their affairs."[40]

UNITED NATIONS INTERVENTION

U.S. recognition of the Yemen Arab Republic did not lead
to a disengagement of external forces or to a reduction in the
fighting. But it did pave the way for the United Nations to
take an active role in resolving the conflict and in reducing
the chances of the struggle becoming more dangerous to world
peace.

The United Nations began actively alleviating the crisis
in Yemen after the State Department declared to news corre-
spondents on January 3, 1963, that:

The United States, as an impartial friend of all
governments involved, remains convinced that the
best interests of the Yemeni people will be served
by the disengagement of foreign military forces and
termination of this external intervention. [41]

The secretary general of the United Nations, U Thant,
dispatched Dr. Ralph Bunche to Yemen on a fact-finding mission.
But, unfortunately, Bunche never visited royalist-held areas.
Before his arrival in Yemen, the Egyptian army had just removed
the royalists from the city of Marib. He was given a rousing
welcome in Sanaa and was taken to the newly "liberated" city
of Marib, where he was greeted with an almost similar reception.
On his return to the United States, he stated that fighting in
Yemen had virtually ceased and mentioned the appalling conditions of the people on the royalist side, which he had not
visited. [42] He also went to Saudi Arabia and to Egypt.

Trips to Yemen by Bunche and by Ellsworth Bunker, both
of whom had gone at the behest of President Kennedy, resulted
in the acceptance of the disengagement plan. Under the arrangement, Saudi Arabia agreed to stop supporting the royalists and
to deny them sanctuary, while the U.A.R. agreed that a United
Nations observation team be sent to Yemen to see that the disengagement was carried out. The United Nations Yemen Observation Mission (UNYOM) was to observe, certify, and report. As
Secretary General U Thant explained in his report to the Security
Council on September 4, 1963, the UNYOM's "operation has no
peace-keeping role beyond observing, reporting, and certify-
ing." [43] The financial cost of the UNYOM was to be shared
equally by Saudi Arabia and the U.A.R. The mission consisted
of 200 Canadians and Yugoslavs, under the command of General
Carl von Horn. It was also agreed that the mission would remain
in Yemen for four months. The mission began on May 4, 1963.
It was hoped that by September the disengagement plan would
be a complete success and that the Yemeni problem would be
resolved.

Eleven weeks after the disengagement plan took effect,
von Horn resigned from his post because of frustration and,
he said, because of lack of cooperation from the United Nations
headquarters and inadequate provision of air and land transport. [44] Von Horn's statement was made evident by the secretary
general when he reported to the Security Council on the functions of the observation mission. He stated that Colonel Pavlovic
and General Rikhe (Thant's military advisors in Yemen) had

"advised me that the present strength of the Mission in personnel
is adequate to carry out its tasks if these are limited to observation and report only."[45] Such a mission could not give necessary
and essential help to the wounded in battle areas, not could it
keep the long borderline between Saudi Arabia and Yemen closed.
The mission was also asked on several occasions to come to the
aid of the wounded in royalist camps, who at that time had no
medical facilities. Moreover, the mission could not investigate
the royalist allegation of the use of poison gas by the Egyptian
air force. Needless to say, U Thant still felt optimistic about
the final result of the mission. The failure of the mission during
the first four months was explained by U Thant in his report
to the Security Council:

> UNYOM Observers have noted departures of United
> Arab Republic's troops in substantial numbers, but
> have also seen replacements arriving, though in
> apparently lesser numbers . . . Observation of the
> Mission to date indicates clearly that in some impor-
> tant respects the terms of the disengagement have
> not been fulfilled by either of the parties.[46]

On October 28, 1963, U Thant declared to the United
Nations:

> . . . that I have no doubt, however, that a continu-
> ing United Nations presence in Yemen of some kind,
> but not necessarily having military attributes, would
> be most helpful and might even be indispensable to
> an early settlement of the Yemen problem, which
> clearly is primarily political and will require a politi-
> cal solution.[47]

This was the first time that anyone had recognized that the
Yemeni conflict was in essence a political problem. This recognition came as a result of strong royalist efforts in stalemating
the conflict and keeping U.A.R. forces embroiled in Yemen.
United Nations efforts to resolve the Yemeni conflict continued in 1964 with no success. The failure of both the United
Nations and the United States to resolve the Yemeni conflict
was because both had concentrated on ways to end Egyptian
and Saudi intervention in Yemen without taking into account
the internal struggle that had provoked the conflict.[48] They
were interested in preserving "peace and security," without
giving too much thought to the Yemeni internal contradictions

that had led to the revolution and to the interventions. The Yemeni problem stemmed from a lack of transformation, or, to be exact, a lack of modernistic tendencies, in the development of the country. When, however, the imamate regime began to move toward modernism through its association with the United Arab Republic and through its acceptance of foreign personnel, it became exceedingly hard, if not impossible, to alter the movement without jeopardizing the system.

INTERNAL IMPACT OF THE YEMENI CONFLICT

As the war in Yemen intensified, its destructiveness became more apparent not only on the land, but also on the Yemeni people, in particular on the tribes. The intensive Egyptian and republican bombings of the royalists' areas in the north destroyed towns and villages as well as crops. The havoc created had never been experienced by Yemen before. The new technologically sophisticated arms introduced into Yemen by the Egyptian forces were far more devastating than Yemen had ever known. The war, coupled with two years of famine (1965-67), almost wiped out agricultural goods and forced both republicans and royalists to import food from abroad.

Since the war was fought primarily by two internal factions, royalists and republicans, tribal allegiance was split. The split of the tribes into two factions disrupted the "traditional pattern of intertribal relationships."[49] The two tribal confederations, the Bakil and the Hashid, that had aided Imam Ahmad in 1948, 1955, and 1959, split into royalist supporters and republican backers respectively. The tribe of Hashid supported the republicans because Imam Ahmad had executed its leading chief and his son for conspiring to overthrow the imamate in 1959. The split was furthered also by traditional tribal values in which some tribes tended to give their allegiance to those in control of their district. However, the greatest disruptor of traditional tribal patterns was the tremendous accessibility of money that was being distributed generously by both Saudi Arabia and Egypt to the tribes in efforts to win their support. The tribes tended to accept money from both sides, and they were willing to switch their allegiance to the party most generous in distributing funds. This trend brought the tribes, some of which had never come into contact with modern elements, into the current of modern living. Thus, for the first time, the tribes witnessed the emergence in their territories of cinemas, refrigerators, and gas ovens. Consequently, they became more conscious of the

shortcomings of their own society. Some of the tribes began
to regard the Egyptians as the vehicle for the new source of
emanation, which, according to Boals, was far stronger than
the emanation of the imam and which the republicans relied on
for success.[50] The Egyptians presented themselves as the new
source of emanation and as the leaders of the movement toward
Arab unity, Arab socialism, and antiimperialism. They hoped
that their emanation would be sufficient to win over everyone
but the most reactionary.[51] However, the tribes saw an opportunity to gather wealth from both the Egyptians and the Saudis.
Material riches, whether in the form of money or arms, inspired
and motivated the tribes to fight. A great many of the tribes
sympathized with the royalists because they were opposed to
the Egyptian presence, which by 1965 was construed as foreign
domination. In time, the value of emanation as presented by
the Egyptians was diluted by heavy-handed Egyptian methods.
This resulted in increases in the ranks of the royalists. Nonetheless, the Egyptian military power was able to keep the royalists
from overwhelming the republic.

The Yemeni society would have undergone changes even
without the revolution. Economic developments had been instituted by Imam Ahmad in 1958. In that year, Yemen granted
the Chinese Communists a concession to build the Hodeida-Sanaa
road. The Soviets were also granted a concession to construct
the port of Hodeida and to build the Hodeida-Taiz road. The
Chinese also built a textile factory, and the Soviets helped to
construct a new hospital in Hodeida. In 1962, Yemen undertook
secret negotiations with the Soviet government for the construction of a huge petroleum storage area in Hodeida that would
have sufficiently served the needs of East Africa.[52] The revolution, however, interrupted the plan. U.S. economic aid was
also furnished in 1959, when the United States agreed to construct the Taiz-Sanaa road. The three major cities in Yemen
were partially linked by surfaced roads when the revolution
began.

The revolution, however, accelerated the process of change.
Yet change would have been rapid even if the revolution had
not occurred. Many supporters of the old regime, including
members of the royal family, had received some form of education
abroad. They would not have permitted the arbitrary rule as
practiced by the imams to be maintained. Their outside education had given them the opportunity to experience a new kind
of life and a new way to change their traditional society into
the contemporary world. Moreover, the roads that were con-
structed during the reign of Imam Ahmad became the instrument

by which the interplay of ideas were communicated. New ideas and new practices made their way to the Yemeni hinterland with relative ease. During the internal war, the roads were used by both royalists and republicans in their endeavors to propagate political and economic concepts. The roads made new ideas easily accessible to places isolated from the main current of modern life.

> . . . it was the roads which began to open up this land, lost for centuries in medieval isolation. Where the roads went, went vehicles, people, goods, new ideas. Tribesmen who had never been outside their own valleys now hitched rides to Sanaa and gawked at the important luxuries from Aden in the shops, went to the movies, relaxed under the bright lights of the cafés and resolved to become city-dwellers. The sheiks in the village could never make the old virtues competitive with the lure of what seemed like modern life in the town. There were young people who saw in the towns an opportunity to escape the restrictive life of their village, to get an education and make themselves modern men. This, indeed, was the trump card played by the republic, by the Egyptians who backed the republic and by the Russians who backed Egypt.[53]

The war in Yemen broke down certain traditional tribal patterns and rejuvenated others that had been submerged by Imam Yahya and Imam Ahmad. Tribal independence was subdued by the Egyptian forces in Yemen. But when the Egyptian military was withdrawn after the Khartoum Agreement in 1967, tribal self-confidence in their ability to govern themselves was once again renewed. A segmented authority prevailed in the country. The republic controlled the urban areas, and its authority was respected. The authority of the republic was missing in areas under tribal control. The tribes governed their areas in accordance with tribal values, and the republic, weak after seven years of civil war, was unable to subject the tribes. Yemen became divided into two areas—republican and tribal.

NOTES

1. George Haddad, Revolution and Military Rule in the Middle East (Santa Barbara: University of California Press, 1974), p. 246.

2. For a detailed account of the night of the coup, see Dana Adams Schmidt, Yemen: The Unknown War (New York: Holt, Rinehart & Winston, 1968), pp. 20-35, and Scott Gibbons, The Conspirators (London: Howard Baker, 1968), pp. 5-25.

3. Haddad, Revolution and Military Rule in the Middle East, p. 235. Haddad asserts that 20 people were executed in the first two days of the revolution. William Brown, "The Yemeni Dilemma," Middle East Journal 17 (Autumn 1963):352. Brown contends that 30 prominent Yemenis were publically executed and that many more were killed.

4. The seven other members who cooperated with Sallal and who were mentioned at the time of the coup were Colonel Hammud al-Jayfi, Major Abdullah Juzailan, Captain Abdul-Latif Daifallah, Captain Mohammed Qaid Saif, Captain Mohammed al-Makhidi, Lieutenant Ali Abdul Ghani, and Lieutenant Mohammed Mufrih. See Ahmad Sharaf al-Din, al-Yaman abr al-Ta'rikh ("Yemen in History") (Cairo: Matba'at al-Sunnah al-Madaniah Abedine, 1963), p. 387. Ibrahim al-Kibsi asserts that Mufrih was not among the group. In his place were Ali Gassem al-Muayyad and Abd al-Ga'wy Hamim. Hamim was the only civilian in the group. Personal interview, October 12, 1975.

5. Sharaf al-Din, al-Yaman abr al-Ta'rikh, pp. 389-91.

6. Haddad, Revolution and Military Rule in the Middle East, p. 253.

7. Howard Wriggins, "Political Outcomes of Foreign Assistance: Influence, Involvement, or Intervention," Journal of International Affairs 22 (1968):217-30.

8. Ibid., pp. 217-18.

9. Ibid., p. 218.

10. Ibid.

11. Ibid.

12. Ibid., p. 219.

13. Charles O. Lerche, Jr., and Abdul A. Said, Concepts of International Politics, 2nd ed. (Englewood Cliffs, N.J.: Prentice-Hall, 1970), p. 116.

14. Ibid., pp. 116-17.

15. Mohammed al-Attar, Al-Takhaluf al-Igtisadi wa al-Ijtima'i fi al-Yaman ("The Economic and Social Backwardness in Yemen") (Beirute: Matba'at al-Wataniah al-Jaza'eriah, 1965), p. 295.

16. Sharaf al-Din, al-Yaman abr al-Ta'rikh, p. 398.

17. Haddad, Revolution and Military Rule in the Middle East, pp. 254-55.

18. United Arab Republic, The Charter (Cairo: Information Department, 1962), p. 11.

19. Ibid., p. 94.

20. Charles D. Cremeans, The Arabs and the World (New York: Praeger, 1963), p. 57.

21. Malcolm Kerr, The Arab Cold War: 1958-1967, 2nd ed. (London: Oxford University Press, 1967), p. 141.

22. Kathryn Boals, Modernization and Intervention: Yemen as a Theoretical Case Study (Ph.D. dissertation, Princeton University, 1970), p. 272.

23. Jay Walz, The Middle East (New York: Atheneum, 1965), p. 128.

24. Boals, Modernization and Intervention, p. 274.

25. In a personal and official reply to my inquiry concerning the YPFU's political aims, Ibrahim al-Wazir explained that the usage of the term "Third Force" came to distinguish the YPFU as neither accepting the republican political ideology nor the royalist form of government. The YPFU desired an Islamic state based on the Shari'a.

26. Boals, Modernization and Intervention, p. 275.

27. Ibid., p. 280.

28. Ibid., p. 281.

29. Robert Stookey, Political Change in Yemen: A Study of Values and Legitimacy (Ph.D. dissertation, University of Texas at Austin, 1972), p. 500.

30. Ibid., p. 501.

31. Haddad, Revolution and Military Rule in the Middle East, p. 278.

32. Egyptian use of poison gas on Yemeni villages was first reported to have taken place on June 8, 1963. In July 1967, the reports were substantiated by the Red Cross. See "Text of the Red Cross Report on Use of Poison Gas in Yemen," New York Times, July 28, 1967, p. 8.

33. U.S. Department of State Bulletin, January 28, 1963, p. 145.

34. Schmidt, Yemen: The Unknown War, p. 186.

35. Ibid.

36. James N. Cortada, The Yemen Crisis (Los Angeles: University of California Press, 1965), p. 7.

37. Ibid., p. 8.

38. Schmidt, Yemen: The Unknown War, p. 189.

39. Ibid.

40. Haddad, Revolution and Military Rule in the Middle East, p. 265.

41. U.S. Department of State Bulletin, January 28, 1963, p. 91.

42. Gerald de Gauny, Faisal (New York: Praeger, 1967), p. 118.

43. U.N. Security Council, S/5412, September 4, 1963, p. 2.
44. de Gauny, Faisal, p. 121.
45. U.N. Security Council, S/5412, p. 3.
46. Ibid., pp. 3-4.
47. U.N. Security Council, S/5447, October 28, 1963, p. 8.
48. Boals, Modernization and Intervention, p. 283.
49. Ibid., p. 256.
50. Ibid., p. 267.
51. Ibid., pp. 275-76.
52. Zaid al-Wazir, Muhawalt li Fahm al-Mashkelah al-Yamaniah ("An Attempt to Understand the Yemeni Problem") (Beirute: al-Sharikah al-Muttahedah lil-Towze'e, 1968), p. 197.
53. Schmidt, Yemen: The Unknown War, p. 287.

6

IDEOLOGICAL CONFRONTATION
AND WAR

The attention of this book has been devoted to the process of political change in Yemen. This chapter, however, is devoted to the rivalry between Saudi Arabia and Egypt for supremacy in the Arabian Peninsula. The contention of this writer is that the Saudi-Egyptian rivalry was primarily a struggle for power, underlined by ideology. It was part of the conflict between traditionalism and modernity in the Arab world.

Modernity, as previously defined, is loosely used interchangeably with the term "Arab revolutionary," because it was the Arab revolutionary regimes that demanded vociferously the alteration of the social, political, and economic structures in the ancien régime.

The significance of the Saudi-Egyptian rivalry was that it influenced the attitude of both states during their intervention in Yemen. Moreover, their rivalry intensified the cleavages that were already manifestly apparent in the Yemeni society, and it enhanced the incoherence. Consequently, both states were incapable of restoring coherence, stability, peace, and justice in Yemen.

The intentions of this chapter are twofold: to evaluate the ideological distinction between modernism and traditionalism, as exemplified by Egypt and Saudi Arabia, and to examine the inability of both Egypt and Saudi Arabia to resolve the Yemeni conflict.

IDEOLOGICAL CONFLICT

In the 1950s, several developments in the Arab world significantly altered the fervor of unity and rivalry in the area.

Revolutionary movements in several Arab states won control
from the traditional elites; one of the first was Gamal Abdul
Nasser in Egypt. From that moment, the struggle between
traditionalism and modernity in the Arab world became intense.
It induced the Arab states to propagate subversion and propaganda warfare against each other. Thus, a revolutionary regime
in one particular Arab state wishing to overthrow a conservative,
traditionalist adversary in another Arab state would call upon
Arabs in Jordan, Yemen, or Iraq to accomplish that task.[1]
This became a political maneuver used by both traditionalist
and revolutionary Arab regimes. At times, the struggle was
personal, between the leaders of the respective regimes. There
were alleged assassination plots against King Saud by Egypt
and against Nasser by King Saud. The struggle "became a
clear function of the struggle and rivalry for domination."[2]
Underlying the struggle were ideological differences.

Traditionalist systems, as exemplified by Saudi Arabia,
are closely related to the leader. The traditionalists consider
the leader (imam, king, and so on) as the patriarch in the system. He dominates his subjects as a parent dominates a household. Power is absolute and only limited by certain traditional
beliefs and religious precepts. The leader rules directly, and
all government administrative agencies function dependently.
They serve the will of the leader and are staffed with retainers,
servants, sons, and uncles of the ruler.

Sovereignty in a traditional Moslem society is vested in
the Shari'a or Islamic law as revealed in the Qur'an. The
Shari'a serves as the basic restriction to the ruler's powers.
Traditionalist regimes have no formal written constitutions by
which the limitations of the ruler are defined and specified.
Since the traditional Arab leader achieves his position by traditional means, he automatically enjoys legitimacy and legality.
Legitimacy implies that, to the extent to which consensus exists,
authority is in the proper hands. Legality, on the other hand,
implies that those in power have achieved authority by legal
means. The traditional leader is, therefore, given personal
control. He is motivated to uphold traditional values over
political and social reforms, as was the case during the reigns
of Imam Yahya and Imam Ahmad. "To permit any innovation or
any form of change, even though it might enhance the ruler's
immediate interest, would damage the very basis of his power."[3]
Only through massive doses of wealth are social and political
changes made in a traditional society. However, the leaders
maintain a fine degree of political control and political authority,
as is the case in contemporary Saudi Arabia.

Traditionalist Arabs are nationalists. Their nationalism is conservative and cautious. Professor Fayez A. Sayegh refers to them as "static nationalists."[4] He asserts that static nationalists "see no need for qualitative change in the basic forms and structure of Arab life."[5] They are satisfied to develop in accordance to their own prescribed formulations.

Like the traditionalist systems, the revolutionary Arab systems revolve around the central figure of the leader, who usually attains power through a military revolution. His overall occupation is to gain legitimacy for his administration and for his newly established political system. He, therefore, institutes parliamentary rules and constitutions. This is not, however, the final stage. Since the revolutionary leader needs to reassert his domination over the state and to maintain a high level of enthusiasm for his revolution, he undertakes "actions capable of reawakening enthusiasm and support for his leadership."[6] The seizure of the Suez Canal by President Nasser in 1956 illustrates such high-fevered enthusiasm. Furthermore, the revolutionary Arab leader, as exemplified by Nasser, strives to give permanent legitimacy to his revolutionary regime. Such an endeavor is usually undertaken through the use of a yes-or-no referendum in which the masses are asked to "legitimize a disguised military dictatorship."[7]

The revolutionary Arab leader, as a "savior of his people," naturally uses Arab nationalism to conceptualize his political system. He appeals to the Arabs as an Arab nationalist whose sole purpose is to regain Arab unity and Arab greatness, presumably under his leadership.

Nonetheless, the revolutionary Arab leader endeavors to create an ideological base through which reforms can be achieved. The adoption of socialism becomes not only the means by which legitimacy for the revolution and the leader is attained, but also a vehicle toward Arab unity.

The pace of social revolution in the Arab world accelerated because of the impact of Western civilization. The application of socialistic principles to the economic sphere was part of that revolution. The movement was intimately connected with the struggle against neoimperialism and neocolonialism, particularly against the establishment of the state of Israel and its ideological base of Zionism.

The failure of parliamentary democracy to implement more democratic social and economic reforms in the traditional Arab states resulted in the discrediting of the ruling elite and of their systems. At the same time, the ideals of a more democratic society, with equal opportunities and shared privileges, were

not discredited but were embodied into the socialistic revolutionary Arab doctrines. For this reason, revolutionary Arab
nationalists have been referred to as "dynamic nationalists."[8]
Socialist doctrines allowing for varying degrees of private
ownership were accepted by the revolutionary Arab regimes.
However, the term "socialist democracy" as used by the Arab
socialist governments referred to systems like those of post-
World War II Eastern Europe. Such systems were characterized
by one-party rule, the violent application of socialist principles,
secret police, and the destruction of the middle class through
the confiscation of the assets and properties of most workers. [9]
The problem that beset Arab revolutionary regimes, and one
that inevitably brought them into conflict with traditional Arab
states, was their assumption that it was their "moral responsibility for establishing justice as the goal of all social action by
the state."[10] They assumed a messianic mission in which their
political ideology was meant to incorporate all Arab peoples.
Michael Aflag, the founder of the Ba'ath Socialist party in Syria,
said in his book al'Ba'ath wa al-Ishtirakiah ("Ba'ath and Socialism") that his socialism was based upon a united Arab people
and that it had always supported the movement toward a complete
Arab unity.[11] According to the Ba'ath socialist ideology, the
state must dominate the individual in order to assert justice.
Thus, rigid and relentless regimentation of the masses was practiced and a policy of strict conformity to the goal of the state
was adopted in most Arab revolutionary socialist regimes.

Socialistic principles in the Arab world had to be made
acceptable on Islamic grounds. Since the ideals of social justice
and equality were not foreign to the Arab/Moslem tradition, and
since Islam dominated the lives of Moslems, socialism and social
justice were not the issues that caused dispute. The issue that
confronted the Arab socialists was the problem of legislation.

According to the traditionalists, legislation in areas not
considered by the Qur'an is permissible. The guiding instrument in legislation is human reason, which must pay due respect
to Islam, and the Shari'a as embodied in the Qur'an. Humans,
according to Islam, are free to adopt their own forms of government and constitutions and to enact their own statutes within
the limits of sovereignty as embodied in the Shari'a, in the nation,
and in the imam. Accordingly, the latter is the guardian of
God's law and the chosen of the people.

The term "chosen of the people" raised differing views
between the traditionalists and the revolutionaries in the Arab
world. It became a basic and fundamental philosophical difference, which underlined the principle of legitimacy. According

to the traditionalists, legitimacy was absconded by the revolutionaries since the revolutionary leaders had never placed their claim to power on the principle of election through consultation (shura). The revolutionaries argued that the traditionalist leaders had so violated the principle of the shura that they could not at all pretend to be legitimate or to represent the will and desire of the whole community (umma) of Islam. According to them, the traditionalists represented only the elite of the community—the privileged few. Social justice and equal opportunity through merit were a sham in a traditional society. The representation of the umma was best realized by a leader capable of expressing the desires and needs of the society. Such a leader, the revolutionaries claimed, could only come from individuals capable of removing themselves from self-centered and reactionary thinking.

While the traditionalist governments upheld the status quo in their regions, the Arab revolutionaries attempted to alter the economic, social, and political stratification of the Arab society on the basis that the Arab world had become defective and stagnant. The revolutionaries were of the strong opinion that Palestine was lost to Zionism in 1948-49, not because the Arab states lacked arms or because the international community stood in opposition to their political objectives, but because the Arab states lacked competent leadership.[12] Moreover, the Arab states were still under the tyranny of domestic forces perpetuating backwardness and hindering progress.[13] The same systems that were responsible for the loss of Palestine were still in existence. As long as they were in control, social change and basic economic and political reforms would not be forthcoming. Arab unity would not be realized. The revolutionaries argued that this was made manifest by the different Arab states championing state-sovereignty over fundamental inter-Arab cooperation in areas important to all Arabs. Furthermore, it was also manifest in the insistence of the traditionalist regimes on maintaining a close relationship with the imperialist Western powers.

Traditionalist Arab systems favor gradual change so that the polity is not disturbed, and thus, traditional patterns are given an opportunity to adapt to change and are not deprived of legitimacy. This gradualist policy is illustrated by the ten-point statement of policy delivered by Crown Prince Faisal on October 31, 1962. Faisal's ideas about social reforms, though conservative in the eyes of Arab revolutionaries, were rather progressive in the eyes of the traditionalists. His program emphasized the need to maintain social and economic develop-

ments in conformity with the Shari'a and the Prophet's Traditions.
Points one and four are significant in that they assert the fundamental needs of tradition:

> (1) Inasmuch as the system of government should be
> a reflection of the development achieved by the
> community . . . the government is prepared to
> develop the community educationally, culturally
> and socially so that it might reach the level that
> would be truly represented in the form of a unified
> system of government calculated to achieve the
> ideas embodied in the sacred law (shari'a) . . .
> It is believed that the time has come for the promul-
> gation of Fundamental Law for the Government,
> drawn from the Qur'an and the Prophet's Traditions
> and the conduct of the Orthodox Caliphs that will
> set forth explicitly the fundamental principles of
> government and . . . the basic rights of citizens,
> including the right to free expression of opinion
> within the limits of Islam and public policy. . . .
> (4) Since the texts of the Qur'an and Traditions
> are fixed and the country's conditions are changing,
> it is imperative to consider important matters of
> state in the light of these changes and in accordance
> with the sacred law. For this purpose it has been
> decided to create a Judicial Council consisting of
> twenty members chosen from well-known jurists
> and 'ulama and whose functions will be advisory
> on all matters referred to it by the state or individ-
> uals.'[14]

The traditionalist Arab is not prepared to break completely
with the past or to accept purely secular legislation that would
replace the Shari'a or traditional patterns and values. The
methods used by the Arab revolutionary in garnering support
for this program are viewed by the traditionalist with repugnance,
as destructive, and as failing to achieve progress as promised
to the people. The traditionalist cites the incapacity of the
Arab military leaders to deliver prosperity and stability. Slogans
often used by the Arab revolutionary tended to be empty of
content. Their purposes were to inflame the emotions of the
masses. To the traditionalist, practical matters ought to be
dealt with pragmatically by proceeding from one problem to
another.

The ideological conflict between traditionalist and revolutionary Arabs was at times so excited that it was construed as divisive to Arab unity and Arab goals. It contributed to mistrust, suspicion, and wrangling between traditionalist and revolutionary leaders in the Arab world. Alleged assassination plots motivated by both traditional and revolutionary leaders indicates the intensity of the conflict. The conflict, as previously noted, was at times personal. This tended to undermine the ideological differences. Each side's passions were excited, and each seethed with malice for the other. Because Saudi Arabia and Egypt were the primary states in the confrontation, their suspicions and jealousies were carried over to their intervention in Yemen. Consequently, they were unable to implement the agreements reached in the course of their intervention.

EGYPTIAN-SAUDI RIVALRY IN YEMEN

The Egyptian-Saudi rivalry in Yemen was the continuation of a rivalry that had begun in the 1950s. The Yemeni Revolution provided Egypt with an opportunity to become active in the affairs of the Arabian Peninsula and to regain pretige lost as a consequence of the dissolution of the United Arab Republic in 1961. Egypt intervened in Yemen confident that its expeditionary force, assisted by the Yemeni Republican Army, would be able to defeat permanently and swiftly a handful of untrained and undisciplined tribal forces. But Egyptian confidence proved premature. Consequently, the Egyptian-Saudi rivalry continued unabated throughout the Yemeni conflict. Nonetheless, the rivalry, motivated by the military events in Yemen and by regional and international politics, went through several changes. The first change occurred in the early stages of the revolution in which both Egypt and Saudi Arabia tried to manipulate world opinion, in particular that of the United States, to their respective views. The second phase occurred in 1965 when attempts at reconciliation were made by both states. This stage was abandoned in the latter part of 1965. It was replaced by an era of confrontation, which lasted until after the Arab-Israeli War of 1967.[15]

Immediately after the revolution in Yemen ousted the imamate regime, Egypt believed it essential to have the Yemeni republic internationally accepted. It was willing to adopt a conciliatory note in order to win international acceptance of the republic. Thus, it accepted the U.S. disengagement plan. But both Egypt

and Saudi Arabia accepted the proposals only because they en-
sured their clients of survival and their own ideological and
political order. "This conciliatory posture was adopted for
political expediency only, and in fact was contrary to, and
thus invalidated by, the prevailing conditions of ideological
polarity, deep suspicion and extreme hostility."[16]

The acceptance of the disengagement agreement resulted
in the recognition of the Yemen Arab Republic (Y.A.R.) by
the United States. U.S. recognition of the revolutionary regime
in Sanaa was immediately followed by United Nations recognition
of the republic as the legitimate government of Yemen. The
military aspect of the conflict was one in which Egypt pursued
a policy oriented toward ending royalist resistance in Yemen.
It was a calculated attempt also at improving the Yemeni republic's
international position as a government in authority and in control of the country. The tour given to Ralph Bunche of the
city of Marib was interpreted by some to show that the Y.A.R.
had asserted its authority in areas previously held by royalists.
It was also meant to incriminate the ousted regime for the appalling
condition of the country.

The second phase of the Egyptian-Saudi rivalry was vastly
different from the first. The change was influenced by the
military events in Yemen and by regional politics.

After international recognition of the Yemen Arab Republic,
Egyptian authorities no longer considered the survival of the
republic in Yemen as fundamental. They believed that a compromise was essential and were eager to disengage their forces
from Yemen. This remarkable turning point in Egyptian thought
came as a result of Egyptian recognition and perception of a
new situation that evolved from a changing environment. Professor A. I. Dawisha asserts that three factors contributed to the
changing attitudes of the Egyptian decision makers.

The first factor was Egyptian awareness that the:

. . . ideological confrontation between the "progressive" and "conservative" camps had, in the wake of
the first summit meeting (early 1964), subsided considerably. The perception of the "battle of life and
death" between socialism and reaction, which had
been a feature of the earlier period, had been gradually replaced by an attitude of tolerance and a tacit
acceptance of the differing political and social system.[17]

Second, in early 1964, President Nasser visited Yemen and was
completely disillusioned by the flagrant corruption and inefficiency

of the revolutionary administration that he was supporting against the royalist "reactionaries."[18] Finally, the failure of the Egyptian offensive in early 1964 and the subsequent successes of the royalist military machine convinced President Nasser that war was futile. Moreover, the cost of running the war was crippling the Egyptian economy.[19]

Regionally, Egypt viewed with alarm Israel's attempt to divert the Jordan water in the latter part of 1963. Egypt sought a calmer intra-Arab atmosphere in order to frustrate Israel's plans. It became exceedingly important for the Arabs to form a unified front in the face of Israel. The Yemeni conflict was to be temporarily cooled. Consequently, Egypt sought to effectively block Israel's plans by calling for an Arab summit meeting in early 1964.

The summit meeting afforded President Nasser the opportunity to reconcile his differences with King Hussein and with King Saud. This endeavor by Nasser led to the resumption of diplomatic relations between Saudi Arabia and Egypt. Moreover, Jordan, which had withheld its recognition of the Sallal regime, gave its formal recognition to the Yemeni republican government. Egypt and Saudi Arabia agreed to meet in September (1964) in Alexandria in order to determine ways to end the Yemeni conflict. However, before their meeting was held, an Egyptian offensive in Yemen, whose purpose was to achieve a fait accompli in northern Yemen by expelling the imam from the country and by ending royalist resistance in the north, was mounted. The apparent failure of the offensive convinced Egypt to recognize for the first time that a political solution was the only way to resolve the Yemeni war. The Egyptian military position in Yemen became precarious. The royalists were able to regain the offensive and to recapture lost territories as well as many Egyptian personnel and large quantities of Egyptian arms.

The Alexandria meeting between Faisal and Nasser was convened with a certain amount of optimism and resulted in a compromise. They agreed to reduce aid to their respective clients and to create a coalition government excluding both Sallal and al-Badr. The significance of this agreement was that Egypt for the first time acknowledged the political existence of the royalists.[20] It also established a precedent by which future meetings between Nasser and Faisal could be held. It paved the way for future attempts toward a negotiated settlement.

Egyptian conciliatory posture was also influenced by the internal dissensions within republican ranks. High republican officials had become weary of the Egyptian military presence in Yemen. Mohammed Zubeiri, Ahmad Numan, Ibrahim al-Wazir, and Abdurrahman al-Iryani became critical of the government

of Sallal and demanded the withdrawal of Egyptian forces from
the country. Two splinter groups were created from the republican ranks, each demanding the withdrawal of Egyptian troops
from Yemen: the Yemeni Popular Forces Union (YPFU), headed
by Ibrahim al-Wazir, and the "Party of Allah," founded by
Mohammed Zubeiri. The latter called for an Islamic republic,
constitutionally limited and neither imamic nor military in nature.
Zubeiri also published a newspaper, The Voice of Yemen.[21] In
April 1965, Zubeiri was assassinated. His opposition as well as
that of the YPFU to the Egyptian presence and to the Sallal
government helped to convince the Egyptian authorities to find
ways to extricate themselves from Yemen. Consequently, they
permitted the Khamir Conference, attended by republicans only,
to convene in April 1965.

The Khamir Conference had as its objective the formation
of a united plan for resolving the conflict in Yemen.[22] Its
original task was to remove Sallal from power, but the moderates
(followers of Ahmad Numan) rejected such an objective in favor
of limiting the authority of Sallal.[23]

The conference resulted in an interim constitution limiting
Sallal's powers. The royalists did not participate in the conference because they believed that it was "never intended to be a
genuine meeting of all parties, but a maneuver by the Egyptians
and their puppets to win support abroad."[24] Nevertheless, the
constitution called Yemen an "Islamic Arab Republic," and it
provided for a republican council of three members and a consultative assembly of 99 members. The assembly was given the
power to nominate the president of the republic and to withdraw
confidence from the cabinet and the republican council by a two-
thirds vote. It also mentioned a "people's congress," a national
defense council, and a judiciary.[25]

Because the conference objected to the arbitrary rule of
Sallal and to the presence of Egyptian forces in Yemen, its
success was immediately doomed. Sallal exiled and jailed many
republicans who attended the conference. It seemed that the
conciliatory period would end at this juncture. However, royalist military successes in the summer of 1965 were instrumental
in convincing the Egyptians to search for new ways to extricate
themselves from Yemen. As a consequence, President Nasser
left Egypt to meet with King Faisal in Jeddah.

Sallal, who had been viewed as the symbol of republican
intransigence, was shipped to Cairo, and Egypt announced that
it would begin to withdraw its forces from Yemen. However,
the Jeddah Agreement made plain a philosophical and fundamental
disagreement between Egypt and Saudi Arabia. Nasser insisted

on the retention of the words "Republic of Yemen," and Faisal
held that the term must be eliminated in favor of the "State of
Yemen."[26] Nonetheless, the Jeddah Agreement[27] called for an
immediate cease-fire, the end of Saudi support to the royalists,
and the immediate withdrawal of Egyptian forces from Yemen.
A 13-month period was alloted for the withdrawal of the troops,
then numbering 60,000. The agreement was to be carried out
in three stages: first, a caretaker government would be set up
in three months; second, a national plebescite would be held to
determine the form of government; finally, Egyptian troops
would withdraw. A meeting of both royalists and republicans
was to be held in the city of Haradh, north of Sanaa, to determine the means by which the objectives of the Jeddah Agreement
would be implemented.

The Haradh Conference was convened on November 23,
1965, under the supervision of the two patron states. The
representatives immediately disagreed on whether the Jeddah
Agreement had intended to abolish the republic and the imamate.

Although the patron states supervised the Haradh Conference, they were unable to establish order. The conference
became overburdened and confused. Insignificant issues became
major. During an entire month, the representatives only met
three times.[28]

Although Egypt and Saudi Arabia were anxious to end their
interference in Yemen, their clients generally were not eager to
see an end to the conflict. Little or no compromise was made by
either side during the Haradh Conference; hence, it failed.
However, it seems logical and reasonable to assert that, had
the two patron states pressured their respective clients to compromise, the Yemeni conflict would have been settled. The
bitter historical animosities between Egypt and Saudi Arabia
could not be subordinated for the sake of peace. Consequently,
the era of conciliation was abandoned in favor of confrontation.

The era of confrontation, like the eras of political manipula-
tion and of conciliation, had several causes. The first was the
military buildup of Saudi Arabia in the latter part of 1965. The
United States and Great Britain made large shipments of jets
and other military equipment to Saudi Arabia. King Faisal negotiated with Britain for the purchase and installation of 37 mobile
Thunderbird ground-to-air missiles.[29] Egypt could not tolerate
a Saudi military buildup as long as it was in a bitter conflict in
Yemen. Moreover, Egyptian authorities were alarmed by the
increasing stability of Saudi Arabia. Under King Faisal, Saudi
reforms were undertaken to improve the living standards of the
Saudi people. The success of the reforms clearly indicated

that Saudi Arabia was maintaining coherency in the system by placating the forces of modernity.

Second, Egypt was fearful of increasing Soviet involvement in Yemen. Soviet interest in Yemen had greatly increased since 1964, when Sallal concluded an agreement with the Soviets for economic and technical assistance. The Egyptians were apprehensive of further Soviet incursions and sought to limit the Yemeni republican government's debt to the Soviet Union by continuing the struggle with greater intensity.

Third, early in 1966 Great Britain announced that it would withdraw from South Yemen in 1968. The announcement influenced Egypt to adopt the "long breath policy" aimed at withdrawing Egyptian forces from the highlands in the north, west, and east of Yemen and at concentrating them in the three-city triangle: Sanaa, Hodeida, and Taiz.[30]

Egyptian adoption of the "long breath policy" may have been motivated by Egyptian defeats by royalists or by the "recognition that an extensive area of inaccessible terrain without efficient communications and administrative network was next to impossible for a limited number of trained men to control."[31] The policy also implied that Egypt foresaw the hopelessness of a military victory over all of Yemen.[32]

By concentrating its forces in the southern part of Yemen, Egypt hoped to easily assist the South Yemeni nationalists in gaining power and in establishing a socialist regime in Aden once Great Britain withdrew. Egyptian departure from Yemen would be politically inappropriate at this crucial juncture.

Finally and most importantly, Egyptian policymakers were alarmed by Faisal's attempt to form an Islamic alliance. Faisal's scheme of developing closer ties with predominantly traditionalist states and with a greater Moslem character became obvious to Nasser in the spring of 1966. According to the Egyptians, Faisal's plans were a direct extension of Western imperialism and a revival of the hated Baghdad Pact. The creation of the Islamic alliance was essentially a diplomatic and propaganda effort by King Faisal. Faisal went on a diplomatic tour to various Arab and Moslem states to enlist support for his alliance. He visited Jordan, Morocco, and Iran. Faisal's trip to Iran angered Nasser because the shah of Iran had been at odds with Nasser for several years. The shah had criticized Nasser's intervention in Yemen and had occasionally slipped arms and money to the royalists. The creation of the Islamic alliance refined the ideological conflict between traditionalism and modernity.

Angered by King Faisal's diplomatic moves and by the increased dissension within republican ranks, Nasser returned

Sallal to Yemen after a nine-month stay in Egypt. The act in itself indicates Egyptian abandonment of conciliation in favor of confrontation. Although the imposition of Sallal on Yemen was a blatant interference in the affairs of a supposedly sovereign state, it demonstrated to the world that Egypt was the foremost authority in Yemen. It further indicated Egypt's frustration over its inability to defeat the royalists and to placate the dissident republicans.

The war in Yemen continued to intensify until after the Arab-Israeli War of June 1967. The massive defeat of the combined forces of Egypt, Syria, and Jordan by Israel shifted the attention of Egyptian policy decision makers from Yemen. It was the prelude to a permanent disengagement of Egyptian forces from Yemen. No longer was ideology the all-important factor in the conflict between Egypt and Saudi Arabia. The immediate need of Egypt was the restoration of its army and its shattered economy in the wake of the defeat. Consequently, Egypt agreed in the Khartoum Agreement of August 1967 to withdraw its forces from Yemen and to revive the Jeddah Agreement. In return, Saudi Arabia agreed to give Egypt the financial support necessary to replace revenues lost through the closing of the Suez Canal. This quid pro quo agreement was satisfactory to both patron states, but their clients were not receptive to the agreement. Sallal rejected the agreement because it was reached without his having been consulted. [33] The royalists contended that Nasser was just stalling for time so that he could recover from the defeat at the hands of Israel. [34]

In December 1967, practically all of the Egyptian forces in Yemen were withdrawn. By coincidence, this occurred only ten days after the British had left Aden. In the same month, Sallal was overthrown by the dissident republicans who opposed his rule. The Yemeni Popular Forces Union did not play a role in the ousting of Sallal. It contended that the new republican regime opposed the creation of an Islamic state whose objective would be the perpetuation of the Islamic Shari'a. Nonetheless, the new government, composed almost entirely of civilians, pledged to open peace talks with the royalists. The royalists, however, had by then lost their effectiveness as a unified entity. They had become split between forces loyal to al-Badr and followers of Prince Mohammed ibn al-Hussein, the leading member of the royal family during the civil war. The split, coupled with the withdrawal of Egyptian forces from Yemen, weakened the effectiveness of the royalists. A great part of the royalist resistance was aimed at the Egyptian presence in the country. Once the Egyptian troops had left, royalist resistance to the republic declined.

While royalist military effectiveness was declining rapidly, the republic was becoming more viable, largely because of help from Syria, Algeria, and the Soviet Union. The Soviet Union was instrumental in assisting the republican army in ending the royalist seige of Sanaa that had been in effect during the last quarter of 1968. The inability of the royalists to capture Sanaa convinced the Saudis that continuous support of the royalists was now a liability. Events in the peninsula had been instrumental in their decision. Not only was the republic showing signs of stability, but it was also apparent that it was the system likely to succeed in Yemen. Moreover, events in South Yemen had progressed considerably since the British departure. The Egyptian-backed Front for the Liberation of South Yemen (FLOSY), which had taken control of South Yemen before the British departed, lost the power struggle with the radical National Liberation Front (NLF), the Soviet-backed party. To the Saudis, the NLF was an outright communist party, and the People's Democratic Republic of South Yemen was viewed clearly as a communist regime. It became imperative for the Saudi government to seek improved relations with the republican regime in Sanaa in order to make possible a unified action against the NLF.

The disintegration of the royalists as a military force may be said to have occurred in the middle of 1969, when the Sanaa-Taiz road, which had been closed by the royalists for 15 months, was opened by the republican forces. In March 1969, Mohammed ibn al-Hussein resigned as the imam's deputy. The cohesiveness of the Hamid al-Din family withered. In October 1969, the last royalist stronghold was captured by the republican forces. After seven years and countless thousands dead, the war in Yemen came to an end.

Traditionalism as a conceptually formulated ideology, however, was not obliterated. It remained a viable force, but it had partially succumbed to the forces of modernity. The creation of the Yemen Arab Republic maintained traditional values, manifested in the Permanent Constitution drawn in 1971.

NOTES

1. P. J. Vatikiotis, Conflict in the Middle East (London: George Allen and Unwin, 1971), p. 90.
2. Ibid.
3. H. B. Sharabi, "Power and Leadership in the Arab World," Orbis (Fall 1963):584.

4. Fayez A. Sayegh, Arab Unity: Hope and Fulfillment (New York: Devin-Adair, 1958), p. 164.

5. Ibid.

6. Sharabi, "Power and Leadership," p. 590.

7. Ibid.

8. Sayegh, Arab Unity, p. 164.

9. "The Arab Middle Class Protests," Atlas (February 1964):110.

10. Sharabi, "Power and Leadership," p. 591.

11. Michael Aflag, al-Ba'ath wa al-Ishtirakiah ("Ba'ath and Socialism") (al-Mu'assasah al-Arabiah li'Iddirasat wa al-Nashr, 1950), p. 128.

12. Sayegh, Arab Unity, pp. 158-60.

13. Ibid., pp. 161-62.

14. Majid Khadduri, Arab Contemporaries: The Role of Personalities in Politics (Baltimore: Johns Hopkins University Press, 1973), p. 98.

15. A. I. Dawisha, "Intervention in the Yemen: An Analysis of Egyptian Perception and Policies," Middle East Journal 29 (Winter 1975):50.

16. Ibid., p. 51.

17. Ibid., p. 55.

18. Ibid.

19. Ibid.

20. Dana Adams Schmidt, Yemen: The Unknown War (New York: Holt, Rinehart & Winston, 1968), p. 207.

21. Zaid al-Wazir, Mu'tamar Khamir ("The Khamir Conference") (Beirute: Ittihad al-Gowa al-Sha'biah al-Yamaniah, 1965), p. 9.

22. Ibid., p. 11.

23. Ibid., p. 14.

24. Yemen Communique, issued by the legation of the Mutawakkilite Kingdom of Yemen, 2 (May 1965).

25. The texts of the interim constitution can be found in al-Wazir, Mu'tamar Khamir, pp. 39-45.

26. Dana Adams Schmidt, "British Foresee Peace in Yemen," New York Times, August 24, 1964, p. 2.

27. The text of the Jeddah Agreement can be found in Zaid al-Wazir, Mu'tamar al-Taif ("The Taif Conference") (Beirute: Ittihad al-Gowa al-Sha'biah al-Yamaniah, 1965), pp. 66-69.

28. Abdullah al-Husni, Mu'tamar Haradh: Watha'eg wa Mahadher ("The Haradh Conference: Documents and Minutes" (Beirute: Daar al-Kitab al-Jadid, 1966).

29. Schmidt, Yemen: The Unknown War, p. 277.

30. Ibid., p. 274.

31. Manfred W. Wenner, Modern Yemen: 1918-1966 (Balti-more: Johns Hopkins University Press, 1967), p. 225.

32. Ibid.

33. "Over Their Heads," The Economist, October 14, 1967, p. 145.

34. Stanko Guldescu, "War and Peace in Yemen," Queens Quarterly 74 (Autumn 1967):484.

7

NATIONAL RECONCILIATION
AND NATIONAL INTEGRATION

The Yemeni dilemma between traditionalists and revolution-
ists, which came to an armed conflict after the revolution in
1962, was not a clash along sectarian lines. True, some revolutionaries, notably Abdurrahman Beidhani, attempted to make
the conflict sectarian whereby the Zeidis were portrayed as
ardent enemies of the Shafi'is. It seemed that the struggle was
being formed along sectarian lines immediately after the revolution erupted. Many Hashemites and supporters of the ancien
régime were executed without benefit of trial, and wholesale
confiscation of the property and assets of those who supported
the old order occurred. These actions by the revolutionaries
were considered by the Yemeni people as distasteful and unjusti-
fied. The attempt to divide the state along sectarian lines failed
because it ignored the fact that many of the prominent members
of the revolution were Zeidis and Hashemites. Mohammed Zubeiri
and Abdullah Sallal were both Zeidis who neither viewed the
Yemeni situation along sectarian lines nor encouraged such a
view. Several factors, political and nonpolitical in essence,
operated to derail the fragmentation of the country. They were
also instrumental in the reconciliation between the royalists and
the republicans.

Yemenis would have rejected the partitioning of their country along sectarian lines or on any other basis. Historically,
Yemenis viewed themselves first and foremost as Yemenis. This
was evident even before the genesis of Islam and its subsequent
acceptance in Yemen. Moreover, the Yemeni had always fought
to assert a single political entity in the state, which had for
centuries been well-defined. Among the Yemenis, a common

Yemeni identity had always been manifestly apparent. It must be recalled that both royalists and republicans fought to achieve control over Yemen under their respective ideological beliefs. The Yemenis looked forward to the continuation of a single political entity irrespective of its political ideology. The royalists and republicans fought because their political ideologies and their objectives conflicted, not because they wished to see an end to the unity of the state. During the course of the war, both sides wished to reconcile their differences. However, they were unable to do so because they were divided on crucial principles. The republicans demanded the preservation of the republic and the exclusion of the Hamid al-Din family from future participation in the government. The royalists wished to rename the state and to retain the Hamid al-Din family. Several times, members from both camps met either formally or unofficially to negotiate ways to end the conflict. On each occasion they failed, largely because both parties were unwilling to compromise on crucial issues. The inability of the two sides to negotiate peace was also abetted by the presence of Egyptian forces in Yemen and by Saudi insistence that help to the royalists would not cease until the Egyptian presence in Yemen was withdrawn. The fact that outside intervention seemed unending influenced the local competing factions to be adamant in their attitudes.

The Egyptian withdrawal from Yemen and the subsequent rise to power of the National Liberation Front in South Yemen altered the problem considerably. Egyptian intervention ended, and Saudi support of the royalists was subsequently curtailed.

Reconciliation was also helped by a regional event. The aftermath of the Arab-Israeli War of 1967 convinced many Arabs that disunity had caused their defeat. Unity in aims and goals became imperative in order to face the Israeli menace and to regain lost Arab territories. Egyptian authorities believed the time had arrived for withdrawal from Yemen. Egyptian withdrawal was deemed essential also in order to gain Saudi financial help to replace revenues lost because of the closing of the Suez Canal. When Egypt withdrew from Yemen, Saudi Arabia lost interest in the Yemeni royalists. They had supported the royalists in opposition to the Egyptian presence and in opposition to the radicalism of the republican regime under Sallal. When, however, Egyptian forces were withdrawn and Sallal was ousted and replaced by moderate republicans, Saudi antagonism toward the republican regime in Sanaa diminished. True, the Saudis maintained their support of the royalists after the Egyptian withdrawal, but it was only to counter the support republicans were receiving from other sources. Saudi support of the royalists in

1968 and 1969 was rather small in comparison with the days when Egypt had had its forces in Yemen.

When the National Liberation Front (NLF) took power from the Front for the Liberation of South Yemen (FLOSY), Saudi Arabia became alarmed. To the Saudis, the NLF represented a communist party. The establishment of the People's Democratic Republic of South Yemen (PDRY) was viewed by Saudi Arabia as the creation of a communist regime. The formation of a communist state in the Arabian Peninsula could not be tolerated by traditionalist Saudi Arabia. It became imperative to the Saudi government to improve its relationship with the republican regime in Sanaa in order to develop unity of action in opposing the South Yemeni regime. The Saudis feared that continual opposition to the republicans in Sanaa might influence the Yemeni regime to move closer to the South Yemenis in an attempt to form a unified front hostile to the Saudi government.

Saudi Arabia was also motivated to bring about reconciliation between the Yemeni royalists and republicans by the fact that it wanted Yemen to attend the Islamic conference scheduled to be held in Jeddah in March of 1970. It was essential to the Saudi government to have the Yemeni regime represented at the conference as a friend, not as an antagonist.

Thus, in early 1970, King Faisal met with representatives of the royalists to inform them that reconciliation was imperative.[1] He urged the members to meet with the republican prime minister to negotiate a reconciliation agreement. The king did not specify whether the republicans would consider discussing the issue of the name of the state, however, rumors circulated before and after the meeting that Faisal had acquiesced to Nasser's appeal to retain the name of the republic. The validity of the rumors can only be conjectured. It can be surmised that King Faisal had accepted the republican demands that the issues of the Hamid al-Din family and the name of the republic were beyond consideration. The Yemen Arab Republic was willing to discuss everything else. The demands of the republican regime were presented personally to King Faisal by Yahya al-Mutawakkil[2] prior to the king's meeting with the royalist leaders. The royalists had to abide by Faisal's proposal.

The reconciliation agreement between the Yemen Arab Republic and the royalists, excluding the Hamid al-Din family, was reached on the basis of amalgamation. Before the two factions met, al-Badr granted his permission to the tribes loyal to him to make their own decisions. He also absolved them of their allegiance to him. Al-Badr then left Jeddah for Great Britain.

The agreement reached between the Yemen Arab Republic and the royalists stressed the principle of national unity. Many royalist leaders were integrated into the Yemen Arab Republican government. The Consultative Council, the parliament of the government, was expanded to accommodate royalist members as well as representatives from areas previously under royalist control. The administration of royalist areas was left under the jurisdiction of former royalists. In accordance with the law, the president of the republic appointed 20 members from the total membership of 159 to the Consultative Council. Ten royalists were appointed to the council. The Republican Council was expanded from four to five to include a royalist.[3] The royalists were allotted four of thirteen seats in the Council of Ministers and three of eighteen ambassadorial positions.

The terms of the agreement were not acceptable to certain elements on republican and royalist sides. Elements in the republican government resisted the agreement on the basis that it offered too much. Some royalists contended that the terms of the agreement did not provide equal treatment. They asserted that republicans outnumbered royalists in all important government departments. However, sentiment among the Yemeni people was in favor of the reconciliation agreement. Soon those who opposed the agreement were pressured into silence.

After the reconciliation agreement was reached, the Yemen Arab Republic sent a delegation to attend the Islamic conference in Jeddah. The Saudi government received the delegation on friendly terms. Yemeni opposition to Faisal's traditionalist ideology ceased to exist. In July of 1970, diplomatic relations between Yemen and Saudi Arabia were restored.

The reconciliation agreement paved the way for future national aims and goals. The fact that the Yemeni problem was, for all intents and purposes, resolved implied that the Yemen Arab Republic could now plan for future national integration that would include South Yemen. No doubt both Yemeni states were separate political entities, each pursuing its objectives along different political beliefs and concepts. The primary factor that convinced the Yemen Arab Republic to formulate the concept of national unity in its Permanent Constitution, drafted in 1971, was the common Yemeni identity.

When the NLF took power in South Yemen, many South Yemenis emigrated to the north to escape its political tyranny. Members of the defunct FLOSY made their journey to the north, and their leaders became active members of the Yemen Arab Republic. A prominent leader of FLOSY served as foreign minister of the Yemen Arab Republic. North Yemeni cities were literally expanded in order to accommodate South Yemeni emigrants. The Yemenis in the north consider South Yemenis as an integral part of Yemen, enjoying the same privileges, opportunities, and equal rights as those born in the north. Largely because the Yemen Arab Republic alleviated the problems of the emigrants from the south by integrating them into the system, friction between it and the South Yemeni regime intensified in 1971. The consequence of the friction was open hostility. The war between the two Yemenis was short in duration and was settled to the satisfaction of both states. Even though both states pursue different values, the fact that they share a common identity is important in the consideration of national unity.

The Permanent Constitution of the Yemen Arab Republic[4] specifies, first, the value of the state. It emphasizes the relevance of Islam. Yemen is declared in Article 1 of the document as an Arab-Moslem state and the Shari'a as the source of all laws. Article 5 declares that "Yemen is an indivisible whole and endeavors to realize the Yemeni unity which is the sacred duty of every citizen."

The constitution, the work of moderate republican leaders, asserts traditional values, taking great care to guard against theocracy or autocracy. It aims to reestablish a decentralized political system. It is significant to note that although the constitution emphasizes national unity, it does not mention Arab political unity. It speaks of strengthening "relations with our brothers, the Arabs" (Preamble). Clearly, this indicates that the Yemen Arab Republic subordinates its general Arab objectives for the relatively more significant local national identity. This, however, does not imply a lack of response to general Arab objectives from the Yemeni leadership. National objectives only take priority over general Arab objectives when the latter are not construed as vital to the Arab nation as a whole.

The Yemeni regime, as constituted after the reconciliation agreement, was unable to pursue its objectives along the principles of the constitution. It was also unable to cope with the problems of administering the state. Tribal disaffection with the central government was to some degree complimented by disagreements between the president of the republic, Abdurrhman al-Iryani, and Saudi Arabia.

When it became evident to the army that political stability was about to be destroyed by the differing factions, it stepped in and took the helm of political authority. Under the leadership of Col. Ibrahim al-Hamdi, the military, in conjunction with the tribes, instituted the "Corrective Movement" in June of 1974 to

regenerate enthusiasm for the republican system and end potentially hazardous friction within the state.

The transfer of power from civilians to the army did not
imply a break with accepted historical values in the Yemeni
society. According to some Yemeni scholars and diplomats, the
Yemeni society is capable of accepting and adapting to political
changes insofar as those changes do not hinder or disfigure
the Islamic context and character of the state. Thus, when
al-Hamdi suspended the Permanent Constitution, no action was
taken by the differing factions (tribes, ulema, and ideologues)
to reverse the process.

During al-Hamdi's presidency, Yemen began in earnest to
develop its economic system by adopting the first Five-Year
Plan (see Chapter 8). It also held itself aloof from East-West
confrontation and began to gradually assert social and political
integration.

NOTES

1. Ibrahim al-Kibsi, who attended the meeting with King
Faisal, asserted that the king reiterated to the delegates the
need to end the Yemeni conflict in order to form a united Arab
front in the face of continued Israeli occupation of Arab lands.
Personal interview, November 15, 1975.

2. Yahya al-Mutawakkil, a Sayyid, was one of the most
important military leaders responsible for the defense of Sanaa
during the seige of late 1967 and early 1968. He was instrumental
in breaking the seige. He later helped to bring about reconciliation.

3. The lone royalist member of the Republican Council,
which acted as the highest executive body in the state, was
Ahmad Shami, former royalist foreign minister.

4. "Permanent Constitution of the Yemen Arab Republic,"
Middle East Journal 25 (Summer 1971):389-401.

PART IV
On
National Growth

8

NATIONAL GROWTH

After suffering the ordeals of a protracted civil war, the Yemeni society was in need of change. Change was introduced by the "open-door policy" adopted in 1971; it paved the way for national growth.

The way to national growth had been a latent and underlying element of the reconciliation agreement between the royalists and republicans. The fact that Yemen was viewed by the outside world as a unified whole in harmony with itself after the implementation of the reconciliation agreement meant that Yemen was serious about improving the lot of the Yemeni society.

The open-door policy gave the impression that Yemen was going to pursue national development. The policy was suited for change.

As an underdeveloped society, Yemen needed international recognition and interest in its attempts to change. To stimulate its society, it had to have financial, technical, and professional assistance from the outside world. Consequently, it improved its relationship with conservative Arab states and with the Western bloc nations.

It is the intention of this chapter to examine Yemen's pursuit of national growth. The analysis focuses on the socioeconomic and political sectors in an attempt to evaluate the policies of the Yemen Arab Republic (Y.A.R.) in developing these spheres.

SOCIOECONOMIC DEVELOPMENTS

Economic development has been defined as the reduction of mass poverty and the increase in levels of consumption for the masses of the populace.[1] It is the ability of the state to produce goods and services per capita and to increase tangibly the standard of living of the masses.[2] As poverty decreases and consumption and production increase, the social awareness of the masses is augmented and enlarged. The demands of the masses on the system become varied and broaden in scope to include political and social issues.

Economic development is not undertaken solely for political reasons. Political objectives play a role in a state's decision to economically expand and develop. However, economic development does cause social change. This is not to imply that social changes lead to modernization. Rather, it means that changes, evolutionary in essence, occur in a society when that society begins to grow economically.

The process of economic development is composed of three kinds of social action: the institution of changes and the acquisition of greater wealth and income, the implementation of institutional changes, and the organization of the social and cultural life of the community so that growth becomes a feature of social change.[3]

By examining Y.A.R. economic development, one may determine the composition of its economic programs and specify the social changes that have evolved.

Yemen's economic circumstances at the outbreak of the 1962 Revolution were lamentable. Attempts by Imam Ahmad to improve the economic condition of the country were far too little and far too late. The strict isolationist policy had deeply harmed the state and made its economic situation difficult to repair.

Although an infrastructure was beginning in Yemen in the 1950s, the revolutionary regime in 1962 "inherited one of the most backward economic structures in the world."[4] Foreigners were aghast to find Yemen literally still living in the Middle Ages. The International Labor Organization in 1967 reported that "social welfare, community organizations, labor welfare organizations, cooperative departments and such institutions were unknown. General and commercial credit, and banking facilities are limited to two towns. . . ."[5]

In light of Yemen's backward economic condition, the Yemen Arab Republic faced an ominous and difficult task. To improve and modernize the country, it needed the immediate financial and technical help of the outside world. The country, at the end of the civil war, was in havoc and general destruction. The agricultural sector was severely damaged due to reductions in livestock and less fertile land.

To alleviate its economic plight, the Y.A.R. opted for a mixed economy—a free-enterprise system with central planning and authority in development. It also improved its relationship with foreign powers in order to gain their support and interest in its development schemes. Thus, it renewed its diplomatic ties with West Germany, which had been broken in 1964 as a result of the latter's close cooperation and support of Israel. It also renewed its diplomatic ties with the United States in the summer of 1972, which was followed by formal recognition of the Y.A.R. by Britain, France, and Holland. These improvements came immediately after Yemen had received regional acceptance on the heels of Saudi recognition in July 1970.

When it appeared that Yemen's relations, regionally and internationally, were improving, it addressed its economic problems. The creation of the Central Planning Organization (CPO) in January 1972 was seen as the first positive effort in that direction. The CPO played a leading role in stimulating the Yemeni economy.

Before the creation of the CPO, Yemen lacked the ability to formulate a coherent policy for development. Yemeni expertise in the technical and administrative fields was very limited. Although this was a heavy burden, the CPO began to recruit specialists and experts not only from neighboring Arab states, but also from the Eastern and Western bloc countries. Planned changes were now to be accepted and enforced. The CPO was given the power to approve the capital expenditures of state enterprises, and it set up 65 planning committees and statistical units in several ministries, state enterprises, and other bodies to increase its effectiveness.[6]

With the technical help of the World Bank and financing by the World Bank and the Kuwait Fund, the CPO was not long in issuing the first development plan, the 1973/74-75/76 Three-Year Development Program. The implementation of the program was a phenomenal undertaking by a country that had not experienced any planned programs in its historical experience. The program was not broad in scope or general in its framework. It was meant to be a beginning toward stimulating the Yemeni economy and creating the framework for future economic planning.

The primary aim of the first Three-Year Development Program was to cultivate the country's infrastructure (roads, electricity, general construction, telecommunication, and irrigation projects). It was believed that development of the country's infrastructure was imperative to further and speedier growth. During this period, industrialization was started. It was on a small scale, but it was a beginning.

Although the Three-Year Development Program introduced modern techniques of development into Yemen, it did not succeed in the vital area of agriculture. Agriculture, as has been stated, is the mainstay of the Yemeni economy. During the three-year program, agriculture grew at a much slower rate than did trade or services. Fifteen percent of the program's allocations were to agriculture. A more significant aspect of the creation of the CPO is that the Y.A.R. initiated new grounds in the institutional area. The Agricultural Fund, the Agricultural Credit Bank, the Tihama Development Authority, research stations, reservoirs, and extension services came into existence.

Despite the fact that not all of the projects initiated in the first Three-Year Development Program were completed, and despite the fact that government assistance was limited, if not absent, and despite the fact that feasibility and engineering plans and studies were almost nonexistent, the program did establish the basic foundation stone for future planning.[7] It served as a framework for the first Five-Year Plan, inaugurated in 1976.

The first Five-Year Plan, 1976/77-80/81, had as its major objectives:

● to improve agricultural production and to work toward self-sufficiency in food. This meant limiting the growing of qat.
● to intensify the industrial sector.
● to improve and modernize the transport and communication sectors.
● to continue to develop the country's human and natural resources.

The objectives were to be realized through a combination of endeavors. Yemen had to induce foreign interest in its proposed projects to gain foreign assistance.

Foreign technical and capital aid was provided on a large scale by international organizations such as the International Development Association, the Arab Agricultural Development Corporation, the U.N. Development Program, the Kuwait Fund, the Abu Dhabi Fund for Arab Economic Development, the U.K. Overseas Development Ministry, and the U.S. Agency for International Development, by countries such as the Federal Republic of Germany, the Netherlands, China, and the Soviet Union, and through the cooperation of the public and private sectors.

The first Five-Year Plan has seen success, however limited. Two factors are seen as reasons for its lack of total success, one regional and the other local.

The regional factor stems from the aftershock of the Arab-Israeli War of 1973 and the subsequent increase in oil revenues. The increase in the price of oil enlarged the treasuries of the Arab oil-producing states. This lead them to allocate huge sums of money to their economic development programs. As an example, $47 billion was allocated for the second Saudi Five-Year Plan. This required Saudi Arabia to engage the experts needed to undertake work on the planned projects. It also required Saudi authorities to recruit the labor force essential to fulfilling the objectives of their development schemes. Consequently, Yemenis were recruited by the Arab oil-exporting states in large numbers. In 1973, the Yemeni labor force in Saudi Arabia was less than 250,000; by 1977, this number had increased to 1,500,000.

Yemen was hurt by the emigration of one-third of its labor force to other Arab states, and it was forced to employ modern technologies. It has increased the use of tractors in two ways: by creating a need for tractors through the shortage and the high cost of labor and by making available the necessary funds through workers' remittances. There are now between 5,000 and 10,000 tractors in the Y.A.R.

Workers' remittances have been more or less responsible for the success of Yemen's efforts at economic development. Because of the remittances, Yemen has seen a balance of payments consistently since 1972. At present, workers' remittances have reached YR$22,625,400,000 (about US$5,000,000,000) since the first Five-Year Plan was inaugurated.[8]

Workers' remittances have increased liquidity in the Y.A.R. through their positive effect on the distribution of income. Generally direct contributions to the families of workers, expenditures of remittances by these families mean income to other Yemenis. However, because Yemenis have not yet become consciously aware of the benefits of investment, they tend to rely on short-term investments with a fast rate of return. They have yet to invest in such long-term projects as industrial and technological enterprises that could conceivably benefit the whole community.

The Yemeni economy has become extremely and, to some, dangerously dependent on workers' remittances. In a personal interview with the prime minister, Dr. Abdul Karim al-Iryani, I asked whether Yemen's dependence on workers' remittances was dangerous to the continued growth of the nation. He replied that the Y.A.R. economic situation dictates that Yemen remain reliant on workers' remittances because they are the only resource that Yemen has in abundance. Yemen, he explained, has no valuable resources to use as alternatives to workers' remittances.

It has no oil nor minerals, and its agriculture is a developing
sector that could in the future be profitable to the Yemeni
economy. Consequently, Yemen will remain dependent on
workers' remittances for some time to come.[9] However, even
the agricultural area will take a long time to develop since much
of the arable lands are being converted to qat areas. The consumption of qat has become a social and economic sickness that
is debilitating national growth. Qat growing has expanded very
rapidly, forcing agricultural resources to be increasingly diverted
to this crop. It owes its popularity to consumer demand, high
prices, and low production costs, and it has become the most
productive cash crop in the state. Its returns exceed those of
competing crops by a wide margin.

The fact that one-third of Yemen's labor force is out of
the country has hindered and, to some degree, hurt its attempt
to become self-sufficient in agriculture. Labor shortage has
also hurt the industrial sector and has increased wages dramatically. To alleviate the labor shortage, the Y.A.R. has been
forced to recruit labor from Pakistan, Egypt, Korea, China,
Somalia, and Ethiopia. As a result, YR$8,718 million has left
the state since 1976.[10]

The industrial sector in Y.A.R. is also hit hard because
it faces high costs; therefore, the cost of the final product is
not competitive either domestically or internationally. Unlike
most underdeveloped economies, which are characterized by
low labor costs and low wages, the Yemeni economic situation
is the reverse. This has prompted many to forecast economic
difficulties for Yemen in both the agricultural and industrial
sectors. The World Bank and other such institutions have
emphasized that because of Yemen's difficulties in achieving
self-sufficiency in agriculture and in lowering costs, competitive
commodities will pigeonhole the economy in a vicious predicament.[11]
They point out that as the country continues to increase its
imports of goods and commodities, workers' remittances will be
consumed within a few years and deficits will not be too far
away. In the first quarter of 1981, Yemen actually experienced
a deficit of US$160 million.[12] However, this was largely caused
by the fact that the government restricted emigration in its
attempt to keep the labor force in the country. This policy was
soon discarded.

The local factor that has limited the success of the first
Five-Year Plan stems from a lack of skills and the traditional
attitudes of the workers in Yemen. Traditional attitudes toward
work for wages among the Yemenis in general are negative.
Consequently, the Yemenis shy away from work, tending to

regard work for wages as demeaning. This partially explains why one-third of Yemen's labor force is outside of the country in spite of high wages at home. Moreover, many Yemenis lack the skills and the knowledge to use new techniques and methods in the agricultural and industrial sectors. The government's attempt to educate the population has not met with a large degree of success because the first Five-Year Plan did not place the development of human resources as a priority. In order to increase the skills of Yemenis, they need to be educated in the technical fields. Recognizing this fact, the prime minister has emphasized that human-resource development will be a priority in the second Five-Year Plan to be inaugurated in 1982.[13]

The first Five-Year Plan has seen outstanding improvement in the transportation and communication sectors in Yemen. All major cities are linked by paved roads. More than 1,200 kilometers of paved roads have been completed by the Highway Authority.[14] This has increased mobility and has opened the country not only to the outside, but also internally. Paved roads have facilitated trade, have eased access to markets for agricultural producers, and have allowed new industries to be established.

Advancements in road construction have been complemented by developments in port facilities, both air and sea. Airports have been modernized in the three major cities (Sanaa, Taiz, and Hodeida). The Sanaa International Airport boasts of its ability to accommodate increased outgoing and incoming cargo. The Hodeida port has been expanded dramatically. From a total capacity of 600,000 tons of throughput of cargo per annum in 1977, the total capacity of the Hodeida port in 1981 for general cargo has been increased to 1,450,000 tons per annum.[15]

Abdullah al-Kurshimi, minister of Labor and Works, was emphatic to me in explaining that the transportation sector has improved tremendously since 1970. According to him, the development of port facilities and roads will continue. He foresees that in a relatively short time, Yemen will develop a transportation system that will dramatically affect the country's overall national growth. To illustrate his point, he declared that the Y.A.R. recently established a new port at Ras Katheb, south of Hodeida. He further reiterated that, for the first time, major sections of the state are linked by easy-access roads.[16]

The development of Yemen's transportation network is both sound and socially admirable. Easy access to remote and isolated areas implies that central authority can be channeled and made apparent with relative ease. It also implies that social, political, and economic integration of the Yemeni community will not be achieved by force. By making services and goods available to all sections of the state, the Y.A.R. is promoting national integration. The prime minister emphasized to me that this is the method that will eventually create respect, loyalty, and obedience to the central authority in Sanaa.[17] As more schools, hospitals, irrigation dams, and wells are made available to the countryside, the rural people will become more dependent on the services of the central government, and this, eventually, will result in social integration.

The communication system is being developed rapidly and is being used significantly to socially integrate the state. Television was first introduced into Yemen in 1972. It has been instrumental in garnering greater social awareness among the people. Yemeni-produced and -directed dramas and plays have emphasized the social ills of the community. News commentaries have accentuated the country's economic efforts and have raised Yemeni awareness and scope of knowledge of the outside world. When Alex Haley's Roots was aired on television, Yemenis tuned in in great numbers, irrespective of the language barrier. The story of Rich Man, Poor Man was also viewed by many Yemenis, indicating that the Yemeni has a great capacity to fathom, perceive, and understand other cultures and attitudes.

As a complement to television, radio and newspaper dailies are reaching the most isolated areas in Yemen. Tribes that once relied upon the spread of news by mouth are now able to hear or read for themselves about events transpiring in their own state and abroad.

Since the Yemeni economy for all practical purposes revolves around workers' remittances coming into the state from Yemeni migrants, this question must be raised: To what extent has emigration affected the social system of the country?

The increased migration of rural males to the Arab oil-producing states has, to some degree, altered the role of women in the agricultural sector. Women are participating more heavily in previously male-dominated agricultural activities such as plowing, planting, and harvesting. Some have taken jobs in industrial firms, such as in the textile complex outside of Sanaa, to supplement what they receive from their male relatives abroad. Moreover, migrant Yemenis who have worked in Saudi Arabia have worked in the industrial rather than in the agricultural sector. Returnees generally tend to go into the industrial sector in search of capital. Consequently, they are demanding more governmental services.

The proportion of Yemeni returnees cannot be tabulated because no census is available. It is assumed that Yemeni emigrants do return, however, for only a short stay. Nonetheless,

those who do return and stay can only be an asset to the state.
Having been exposed to various forms of skills, such as mechani-
cal engineering, carpentry, electronics, and auto mechanics,
they become a constructive element in Yemen's economic and
social mobility. However, this element has negatively affected
the agricultural sector since many rural males have moved into
the cities in search of capital. All cities have seen an increase
in population of between 7 and 12 percent. The 1980 census
taken by the Yemeni government tabulated the inhabitants of
Sanaa at more than 300,000 people, an increase of 165,000 from
the 1975 estimated figure of 135,000.

Internal migration from the rural areas to urban centers
is primarily a male movement. The strong labor demand created
as a consequence of growing economic activities in urban centers
is largely responsible for a decline in the population of rural
areas, for further straining the traditional values within the
Yemeni home, and for adding to the altering role of women.

Yemen's socioeconomic changes have also been affected by
progress in the educational sector.

Mention has been made that in prerevolutionary Yemen,
education was backwards. There were only three high schools
in all of Yemen, with no curriculum of any kind. Yemeni students
going abroad for education had to enroll in high schools in order
to take the science courses they had not had in Yemen. In
prerevolutionary Yemen, secular education was anathema. This
attitude changed with the revolution.

The educational system in the Y.A.R. was broadened and
made to conform to international standards. Schools were opened
in all regions of the state. The number of primary and secondary
schools increased from 700 in 1969/70 to 2,534 in 1979/80.[18] The
University of Sanaa was established in 1971 with an initial enrollment of 61 students and with three schools: the Faculty of Law
and Shari'a, the Faculty of Sciences, and the Faculty of Arts.
The number of students gradually increased to more than 4,000
in the academic year 1980/81 with two new schools: the Faculty
of Commerce and Business and the Faculty of Education. The
university included among its 109 faculty staff 12 Yemenis.
Thanks to financing by the state of Kuwait, the university is
developing rapidly. A school of medicine is in the planning
stage, financed and promoted by Kuwait. It is hoped that the
school of medicine will be ready in two years. Moreover, schools
of engineering and of agriculture are now in the planning stage.

More significant in the development of the educational system is the fact that women are increasingly being encouraged
to enroll. Room and board are provided by the university as
incentives for women to enroll.

This trend is leading to a change in the value structure
of the Yemeni family. As more women are educated, their
demands on the state, in general, and on their families, in particular, become broader in scope. The state is attempting to
use this labor force by encouraging women to work. The faculty
of Education at Sanaa University, as an example, guarantees
its women graduates teaching jobs. However, the state's ability
to absorb high school and university women graduates is limited.
Women, as a consequence, are moving toward the private sector
for jobs.

In social terms, women's active participation in the education
and job sectors has been profound. The fact that women attend
schools along with men, even at the university level, and work
alongside men has considerably eroded old values concerning
the role of women in the Yemeni society. The activities of women
have induced families to be more responsive to women's demands.
The trend is likely to continue. This is not to suggest that
traditional social values are crumbling, but that new values
and inputs into the system are being adopted, at times out of
necessity and at times out of common sense.

Necessity requires the Yemeni family to permit its daughters
to work alongside men for two reasons: the high cost of living
creates the need to supplement family income, and few institutions, public or private, hire only women. Common sense dictates
to a Yemeni family that women must be educated and trained as
long as that education and training conforms to established values.
Social congregation between the sexes, in or out of schools, is
not accepted. The conduct of women and men, even at the
university level, is carefully scrutinized. Within the compounds
of the university, strict codes of conduct for both male and
female students are observed.

In light of Yemen's economic growth, the country has seen
a remarkable expansion of foreign and domestic trade, of government services, of the transportation and communication sector,
and of the educational system. This should not distract from
the fact that Yemen continues to face many problems as an underdeveloped country. "Productivity levels are still extremely low,
especially in agriculture which occupies about three-fourths of
the resident labor force."[19] Yemen's Gross Domestic Product
grew at an average rate of between 8 and 9 percent per year
from 1969-76 and at relatively the same rate from 1976 to 1980,
but this does not preclude the fact that Yemen's products are
relatively poor in comparison with imported manufactured goods.

Yemen's economic progress has had its impact on the country's social system. Rural and urban areas have been forced

to adapt to change, whether derived through uncontrolled circumstances or otherwise. Even though social change is occurring
at a slow rate, there are the beginnings of a traditional backlash,
as exemplified by the Moslem Student League. This association,
recently formed, has begun to articulate its demands on the
state, particularly on the educational system. It has demanded
that women be veiled and that a strict adherence to male/female
separation be observed. It is too soon to declare whether the
league will evolve into an organized pressure group with the
ability to constrain social changes.

POLITICAL DEVELOPMENT

The socioeconomic growth of Yemen, as in most societies,
is closely related to political stability. It is through stability
that continuity and growth are asserted. When stability is disturbed, the system loses its equilibrium and becomes endangered.
The Yemeni political system is relatively new. It was born
in 1962 as a consequence of the revolution. Since then, it has
gone through the trial of time and has shown itself able to survive. It has also increased its legitimacy.
In order to analyze Yemen's political development, Gabriel
Almond's theory on the development of political systems is useful.
It is by evaluating how the political system is able to meet challenges, changes, and diversifications that strain the existing
culture and structure that one may postulate Yemen's political
development.
According to Almond, there are four problems or challenges
to a political system. The first is state building. It is the problem of penetration and integration. The second is nation building.
It is the challenge of loyalty and commitment. The problem of
participation is the third stage. It is the attempt by the political
system to permit the masses to take part in decision making.
The fourth is distribution. It is the pressure to force the political system to redistribute income, wealth, opportunity, and
integrity.[20]
The questions that need to be asked: How has the Y.A.R.
met these challenges and problems? Has it been successful in
overcoming the obstacles inherent to accomplishing the stages
of political development?
Mention has been made that the Y.A.R. has achieved remarkable economic growth under the first Three-Year Development
Program and the first Five-Year Plan. Under these two programs,
goods and services became accessible to the masses. Opportuni-

ties to share in the development of the state were broadened to
include women. Wealth, largely derived from workers' remittances
and foreign aid, went into expanding the economic system, making
it more responsive to public demands.

However, attention must be turned to evaluating Yemen's
attempt at state building, nation building, and participation.

In regard to state building, the Y.A.R. has been successful
in maintaining itself and in surviving international threats to
its political system. It must be recalled that Yemen fought a
civil war for approximately eight years. It withstood royalist,
regional, and international pressures. Another significant aspect
of Yemen's state building is the fact that the system was able to
restore a semblance of continuity when, in June 1974, the military,
in conjunction with the tribes, ousted Abdul Rahman al-Iryani
from the presidency. This act reinforced the system, which
was being challenged and pressured from within. The system
was also rocked two other times, in 1977 and in 1978.

In October 1977, President al-Hamdi was assassinated by
"unknown elements."[21] This act was not only traumatic, but
also deeply felt by the Yemeni people. Al-Hamdi had been able
to gain popular support. He had been instrumental in providing
Yemen with a relative degree of stability, with economic advancements, and with regional and international respect. His policies
were culminated in his official visit, the first by a Yemeni head
of state, to France. Al-Hamdi's successor, Colonel Ahmad al-
Dhashmi, was also assassinated, in July 1978.[22] These two
reprehensible acts of violence shook the political foundations
of the system. It did not, however, collapse. The current
president of the Y.A.R., Colonel Ali Abdullah Saleh, has pursued
a policy similar to those of his predecessors. Consequently,
continuity has been preserved and relative harmony has been
maintained.

The Y.A.R., as constituted in the Permanent Constitution,
was unable to withstand the pressures generated from within
the polity. Administratively, the government lacked the qualified
people necessary to assist a recently formed political system in
performing with equity. It became imperative for the military
to take control of the political system.

In order to placate those who had articulated their grievances
against the political establishment, the military regime of Ibrahim
al-Hamdi instituted the "Corrective Measure" in June 1974. This
act was also meant to increase the viability of the political system
to give the new regime a sense of legitimacy, and to expand its
authority. The "Corrective Measure" created the "Committee of
Correction" to oversee the abolishment of graft and illegal acts.

Subcommittees, under the control of the "Committee of Correction," were established in all the regions of the state. The establishment of this institution was one form of creating new structures and organizations designed to penetrate society in order to regulate behavior and to draw a larger volume of resources from it.

In regard to the element of nation building, people transfer their commitments and their loyalty from small tribes, villages, ethnic origins, or social groups to the central political system. This factor is being achieved in the Y.A.R. in conjunction with economic growth. Mention has been made of the fact that goods and services are being made available to remote areas of the state. The construction of a road network that will reach isolated areas is being viewed by government authorities as a means to achieve loyalty and to transfer commitments to the central government. Loyalty of the Yemeni people to the central government means adherence to values and beliefs essential to the polity by the political system. This somewhat explains Yemen's close attachment to preserving and upholding religious values. It also explains why it upholds a partially free enterprise system and why it tries to assert freedom of thought. The government sustains these elements not only because they legitimize it, but also because they constitute survival for it. It has shunned unification with the People's Democratic Republic of Yemen (PDRY) because the two systems are diverse in political thought, economic practices, and ideological stands. While the Y.A.R. is a decentralized political system, the PDRY has a hierarchical, Marxist political organization. Also, while the Y.A.R. has a mixed economic arrangement, the PDRY has a socialist economic system. In ideology, the two political systems conflict. The Y.A.R. adheres to an ideology that has its roots on traditional and religious values. This does not imply that it upholds the tenets of the shura, but it does give it lip service. On the other hand, the PDRY is a Marxist-oriented system. It sustains a political ideology alien to the masses. These differences have resulted in making unification of the two Yemens an ideal.

It is true that the Yemeni people consider themselves as one society whose roots go back prior to the advent of Islam. It is this belief of wholeness that has made the Yemenis look forward to unity. The foreign minister of the Y.A.R., Ali Lutf al-Thawr, condensed the Yemeni feeling on unification by stating, "The Yemeni has not despaired in his attempts to gain unity. He shall continue his struggle to fulfill this objective. All obstacles before him, whether ideological, economic, or political, will not hinder his historic duty."[23]

The third element in the stages of political development is participation. It involves increases in the volume and in the intensity of demands. It has a tendency to create political groupings or factions, and it challenges the political system to develop according to competence and responsiveness. The Y.A.R. has attempted to infuse this factor into the masses.

Recognizing that unification is the desire of all Yemenis, the Y.A.R. has encouraged the masses to discuss, openly and otherwise, the challenges of unification. It has also created official and unofficial committees to evaluate the element of unity. The ulemas have been vociferous in their discussion of unification. They have not only presented their case on television, but also have written about it in the official organ of the state, al-Thawra.

Their point of view is that unity with South Yemen at this juncture is not feasible because of the apparent discrepancies in the two political systems. The tribes have also used the mass media in asserting their stand. All groups and factions in the Y.A.R., however, speak in favor of unity. They recognize that unification for Yemen will mean greater control of Bab al-Mandab Strait and greater influence in the flow of international commerce going in and coming out of the Red Sea. It also will imply a larger population, increasing it from 8.5 million[24] to a purported 11 million. This will not only increase its regional influence in the area, but also will make it the second most populous nation in the Arabian Peninsula next to Iraq.

A more significant attempt by the political system to increase mass participation and, hence, to win greater loyalty and commitment from the Yemenis, was the drafting of the National Charter. It is a document of objectives and aims.[25]

Divided into six chapters, the charter outlines the objectives, both domestic and international, of the Y.A.R. It was made available to the citizenry, who were asked to evaluate its contents. The state held seminars and encouraged the people to voice their opinions on the charter. Tribes and other political groups were also asked to articulate their views.

It is interesting to note that the charter attempts to reinforce the Islamic character of the Yemeni society. It refers to Islam as a belief and as a way of life. The charter emphasizes the "material, spiritual, philosophical, political, economic, and social" lives of the community.[26] It also asserts that the idea of a charter did not evolve from the top; neither is it a political thought of a particular group wishing to superimpose itself on society and to force society to accept its particular Islamic belief.[27] As to loyalty, the charter declares it to be a religious duty. It insists that participation by the masses in the political decision-making process guarantees democratic rule and prevents tyranny from evolving.[28]

What is intriguing in the charter is that it includes a chapter on Yemen's foreign policy. It recognizes Yemen's historical and cultural bonds with the rest of the Arab states. Priority is given to the Palestinian cause as the most immediate problem facing the Arab world.[29]

The charter clearly defines Yemen as a member of the third world, neutral nations. This is not a break with the past. Yemen's neutrality in East-West conflicts was established by Imam Ahmad in 1954. The revolution of 1962 did not alter this foreign-policy decision. On the contrary, it reinforced it. Yemen is well aware that it is a small, underdeveloped state in need of outside assistance. Neutralism guarantees for it the ability to practice independent choices, arrived at independently, without coercive pressures from abroad. To illustrate this point, the United States shipped to Yemen US $390 million worth of weapons in March 1979 to stem the advances of South Yemeni forces in their three-week border war. The weapons were made available at the behest of Saudi Arabia, which distrusts leftists and views their assertiveness as a danger to the stability of the Arabian Peninsula. Shortly after the delivery of the U.S. arms to Yemen, the Y.A.R. bought a huge shipment of Soviet weapons. This action by the Yemeni government confounded and embarrassed the U.S. government. However, when viewed from a different perspective, the act in itself only underscores Yemen's close adherence to positive neutrality and to its freedom to independently choose and select. The Y.A.R.'s former prime minister summarized Yemen's reasons for purchasing Soviet arms: "We always used Russian arms. We do not, however, feel that this particular policy means we are enemies of the United States. Our principles have always been those of positive neutrality."[30] The foreign minister of the Y.A.R., ali Lutf al-Thawr, has reiterated that Yemen's policy of positive neutrality is a traditional national objective. It is beneficial and is so regarded.[31]

Mass evaluation and examination of the National Charter has clarified ambiguous terms. It has also generated an awareness of its discrepancies.

The Yemeni public is still scrutinizing the charter. The question that is persistently and consistently raised: "Why do we need a 'National Charter'?" The ulemas, the tribes, and the technocrats have voiced their opinions on it. Some have declared it senseless—incompatible with Islamic traditions. They point out that the state does not need to fabricate a document in search of an ideology or of a program of objectives. The Qur'an, they

assert, contains both the means and the objectives for the state.
It is an ideology that governs the political, social, and economic
sectors of society. The Shari'a, as the embodiment of Islam,
is a sufficient instrument in achieving the state's objectives.
Adherence to the Shari'a will guarantee loyalty and commitment
to the state. Implementing the shura will prevent the rise of a
dictatorial and tyrannical rule.

However, the value of permitting the Yemeni masses to
examine the National Charter can be said to be an ingredient
of nation building. The masses, however, are being asked to
decide on the structural form of the charter, not on its substan-
tive framework. Since the charter does not mention the reasons
for its formulation, it cannot be taken as a serious endeavor by
the leadership to expand the flow of trust between the leadership
and the masses.

NOTES

1. Jacob Veirer, International Track and Economic Development (Oxford: Clarendon Press, 1955), p. 125.
2. Harvey Leibenstein, Backwardness and Economic Growth
(New York: John Wiley, 1957), p. 10.
3. John L. Finkle and Richard W. Gable, Political Development and Social Change (New York: John Wiley, 1971), p. 195.
4. Statement delivered by the leader of the Y.A.R. delegation, Fouad Mohammed, minister of Development and chair of
CPO, to the review meeting of the Substantial New Program of
Action of the LDCs of Asia and the Pacific, Vienna, April 8, 1981.
5. International Labor Office, Report to the Y.A.R.
Government on Prospects of Small Industries (Washington, D.C.:
International Labor Office, 1967), p. 2.
6. World Bank Country Study, Yemen Arab Republic:
Development of a Traditional Economy (Washington, D.C.:
World Bank, 1979), p. 55.
7. Abdul Karim al-Iryani, "al-Tanmiah al-Igtisadiah wa
al-Kiddah al-Khamsiah fi al-Gomhoriah al-Arabiah al-Yamaniah:
Dirassah Tahliliah" (Economic Growth and the First Five-Year
Plan in the Yemen Arab Republic: An Analytical Study), Journal
of the Gulf and Arabian Peninsula 6 (April 1980):94.
8. Figure provided to me by Ali Abdullah Ali, economic
advisor to the Central Planning Organization.
9. Personal interview, June 5, 1981.
10. Figure provided to me by Ali Abdullah Ali of the Central
Planning Organization.

11. World Bank, Yemen Arab Republic, p. 53.

12. Figure provided to me by the Central Bank of the Y.A.R.

13. Personal interview, June 5, 1981.

14. Figure furnished to me by the Highway Authority.

15. Figure furnished to me by the Highway Authority.

16. Personal interview, May 28, 1981.

17. Personal interview, June 5, 1981.

18. Y.A.R., Thamaniah-Ashar min Omar al-Thawra ("Eighteen Years in the Life of the Revolution") (Sanna: Ministry of Information and Culture, 1980), p. 136.

19. World Bank, Yemen Arab Republic, pp. ii-iii.

20. Gabriel Almond and G. Bingham Powell, Jr., Comparative Politics: A Developmental Approach (Boston: Little, Brown, 1966), p. 35.

21. Official statements referred to the assassins as "corrupt and destructive elements." Investigations undertaken by the Y.A.R. government to determine who was responsible for al-Hamdi's assassination did not come to any conclusive results.

22. Al-Ghashmi was assassinated by a South Yemeni who met the president on the pretext that he represented the president of the PDRY.

23. Personal interview, May 28, 1981.

24. Thalathat-Ashar Unio (Sanaa: Ministry of Information and Culture, 1981).

25. Y.A.R., Mashrau: al-Mithaq al-Watani ("Program: The National Charter") (Sanaa: 1980).

26. Ibid., p. 23.

27. Ibid., p. 26.

28. Ibid., p. 32.

29. Ibid., p. 76.

30. Georgia Anne Geyer, "Yemen: A Puzzlement That Isn't," Los Angeles Times, March 20, 1980.

31. Personal interview, May 28, 1981.

PART V
Conclusion

9

CONCLUSION

The Yemeni historical experiences since 1918 have been
analyzed throughout this book. Changes in the system have
occurred at times very slowly and at other times quite rapidly.
The changes were largely caused by contradictions within the
polity.

Initially, the contradictions in Yemen stemmed from the
desire of the political system to remain isolationist while importing
new methods into the system, thus provoking a conflict of interest between the new and the old. The persistent refusal of the
imamate to infuse the system with modern techniques and ideas
gave rise to splinter groups that, at first, demanded political,
economic, and social reforms. When those reforms did not
materialize, some of the splinter groups became resistance
movements. The movements did not demand the demise of the
imamate. They attempted to convince the imamate regime to
undertake reforms. When, however, those reforms were not
forthcoming, the movements' political objectives were altered.
They articulated their demands from, at first, Aden and, later,
from Egypt. To them, the imamate had become inefficient, incapable, and incompetent, and it was imperative to alter the
political system.

Allied with Egypt's President Nasser, the Free Yemeni
Movement worked for the overthrow of the imamate. The 1962
Revolution did bring an end to the imamate, but it also brought
havoc and destruction to the Yemeni society, unlike any it had
experienced before. Nonetheless, the Yemen Arab Republic
(Y.A.R.) withstood both the internal and external pressures.
It was able to defeat the traditional forces, represented by the
royalists, who wanted to restore the imamate. When it became

apparent that the republic was to be the political system of the future, the royalist cause was defeated.

During the Yemeni civil war, regional and international interventions and interferences occurred consistently. Saudi Arabia and Egypt were involved directly in the civil war. Each had its client, and each pursued aims and objectives contrary to the other. It did at one time seem that the Yemeni conflict would not end. There were too many outsiders involved, each representing a political and social ideology. However, the primary antagonists in the Yemeni dilemma were the traditionalists, represented by the royalists and by Saudi Arabia, and the revolutionaries, represented by the republicans and by Egypt. Other Arab states that took sides in the conflict were influenced, to a large degree, by their political and philosophical links with the two contending forces. Thus, Jordan supported the royalists while Iraq supported the republicans.

When the reconciliation agreement between the royalists and republicans was formulated, it brought an end to the Yemeni civil war and terminated royalist resistance. It was followed by Y.A.R. adoption of the "open-door policy," which served as the forerunner to Yemeni programs for national growth.

National growth in the Y.A.R. has been fruitful, especially in the transportation, education, and communication sectors. However, it has not been able to reduce the dichotomy of conflicting interests between the traditionalist forces and the forces for radical change. On the contrary, changes within the social structure, although caused to some degree by male migration to the outside, have aggravated the discord between the two groups.

Yemen's open-door policy is, on the one hand, an asset, and, on the other hand, a liability. It is an asset because it has promoted economic advancements. It is a liability because those advancements imply a huge influx of foreign personnel whose ideas and moral ethics conflict with Yemeni traditional values. As East Asian and European workers and experts enter the country, they come face-to-face with a society that is still apprehensive about values contradictory to theirs. Here lies the dilemma for the political elite. Should the state pursue a policy that may aggravate the existing contradictions? Or should it adopt a policy more in conformity with gradual change? The prime minister of the Y.A.R. expressed to me his views on this particular problem by stating that the conflict between traditionalism and revolutionary forces is not as rigorous as it was in the 1950s and 1960s. The Arab people became less political once the issues of independence and freedom were achieved. The political authorities do not as before exploit mass sentiments to arouse popular enthusiasm for a particular political problem. Consequently, conflicting interests between traditionalists and revolutionaries have been subdued. The state of Yemen is pursuing policies that are not deemed risky to its sociopolitico-economic systems.[1]

The essential element in Y.A.R. advancement policies is the belief that time is on its side. Political and social integration are not pursued by force. On the contrary, the state seems to be oblivious to creating a viable nation, integrated and able to authoritatively allocate resources in all its regions. It is heavily dependent upon economic advancements to produce and gain integration. This policy is contrary to past historical practices. The imamate forced integration through the use of arms and the hostage system. Although this policy was reprehensible, its end result was that the state's authority was respected in all the regions. This is not to imply that the Y.A.R. should adopt a similar policy. On the contrary, political integration can feasibly be achieved through the transportation of the consciousness of the Yemeni people. Qualitative changes in the administrative, economic, social, and political sectors of the system, if pursued gradually on the basis of respect for traditionally held values and beliefs, will be more constructive. Yemeni unity with the People's Democratic Republic of South Yemen (PDRY), when achieved, will be a qualitative change since it has been pursued with mass participation.

Integration of the Yemeni society is a difficult task. There are too many weaknesses inhibiting national integration: ideological differences between the Y.A.R. and the PDRY, tribal identity, economic dependency on resources outside the control of the state (workers' remittances and foreign aid), and rivalry between the new and the old. A more significant factor hindering national integration of north and south Yemen is the fact that both political systems have experienced political assassinations and political disturbances resulting from power struggles. The PDRY, like the Y.A.R., has seen the onus of political rivalries damage its prestige internationally and curtail its attempts to develop. In 1977, the country was engulfed in a civil war as a consequence of the political rivalries between Salim Ali Ruhya, president of the PDRY, and Abdul Fatah Ismail, secretary general of the Marxist party. It ended quickly, but only after it had surgically divided the state into two conflicting camps. In the process, many lives were lost.

The violent events in both the Y.A.R. and the PDRY have infused the two political systems with certain misgivings. This has increased incoherence in both systems.

The Y.A.R. is attempting to adhere to the nomos, and, in so doing, it is gaining greater legitimacy. By propagating traditional values and precepts, the Yemeni political system seems to be more conscious of the values of justice. Its radical conduct, influenced by revolutionary rhetoric, has subsided considerably. No longer does it feel paranoic. It is accepting, or at least it is trying to accept, opposing views. Its moderation internally and externally has been instrumental in convincing the Yemeni intelligentsia residing abroad to be less antagonistic and more sympathetic to it.

Yemen, however, is still far from national integration. National integration is not a formidable task. It can be achieved when those in power realize a new form of consciousness constituted in the "awareness that there are patterns and concepts, that these patterns have been developed by man, that these patterns are breaking, and that they can be transformed by man."[2] Transformation and change include creativity that accomplishes or maintains coherence.[3] In order for national integration to evolve, common ground must be achieved among the various factions in Yemeni society, including Yemenis outside the state. Coherence implies stability, and stability cannot be reached unless, and until, justice for all Yemenis is instituted. The state must be made responsive to the demands of the masses, paying greater attention to cherished traditional values. The continuity and growth of the political system depends upon this important variable.

NOTES

1. Personal interview, June 5, 1981.
2. Manfred Halpern, "A Redefinition of the Revolutionary Situation," Journal of International Affairs 23 (1969):69.
3. Ibid., p. 71.

BIBLIOGRAPHY

PRIMARY SOURCES

Abd Allah, Abd al-Illah. Nuskhat al-Thawrah fi al-Yaman: Wath'eg wa Murasalat ("Relapse of the Revolution in Yemen: Documents and Messages"). Damascus: Damascus Palace, n.d.

Hanna, Sami A. Arab Socialism: A Documentary Survey. Los Angeles: University of California Press, 1962.

Heikal, Mohammed H. The Cairo Documents. New York: Double-day, 1973.

Hickenbotham, Sir Tom. Aden. London: Constable, 1958.

Hurewitz, J. D. Diplomacy in the Near and Middle East 1914-1956. New York: Van Nostrand, 1956.

al-Husni, Abdullah. Mu'tamar Haradh: Watha'eg wa Mahadher ("The Haradh Conference: Documents and Minutes"). Beirute: Daar al-Kitab al-Jadid, 1966.

International Labor Office. Report to the Y.A.R. Government on Prospects of Small Industries. Washington, D.C.: International Labor Office, 1967.

Iryani, Abdul Karim. Personal interview. Sanaa, June 5, 1981.

Khalil, Muhammed. The Arab States and the Arab League. Beirute: Khayats, 1962.

al-Kibsi, Ibrahim. Personal interview. Washington, D.C., 1975 and 1976.

Kurshumi, Abdullah. Personal interview. Sanaa, May 18, 1981.

Mohammed, Foriad (minister of Development and chair of CPO). Statement to the review meeting of the Substantial New Program of Action of the LDCs of Asia and the Pacific. Vienna, April 8, 1981.

al-Munjad, Salah al-Din. al-Yaman wa al-Muttahedah bain al-Ittihad wa al-Infisal ("Yemen and the United Arab Republic between Unity and Disunity"). Beirute: Daar al-Kitab al-Jadid, 1962.

Nasser, Gamal Abdul. The Philosophy of the Revolution. Cairo: National Publishing House Press, 1963.

"Permanent Constitution of the Yemen Arab Republic." Middle East Journal 25 (Summer 1971).

al-Thawr, Ali Lutf. Personal interview. Sanaa, May 23, 1981.

United Arab Republic. The Charter. Cairo: Information Department, 1962.

United Nations Security Council Documents. Selected issues (1957-65).

United Nations Treaty Series. (1955-72).

United States Department of State Bulletin. Selected issues (1962-66).

Von Horn, Carl. Soldiering for Peace. New York: David McKay, 1967.

al-Wazir, Ibrahim. Personal reply to questions asked concerning the political program of the Yemeni Popular Forces Union. November 6, 1975.

al-Wazir, Zaid Ali. Mu'tmar Khamir: Nusous wa Watha'eg ("The Khamir Conference: Texts and Documents"). Beirute: Ittihad al-Gowa al-Sha'biah al-Yamaniah, 1965.

_____. Mu'tamar al-Taif: Nusous wa Watha'eg ("The Taif Conference: Texts and Documents"). Ittihad al-Gowa al-Sha'biah al-Yamaniah, 1965.

World Bank Country Study. Yemen Arab Republic: Development of a Traditional Economy. Washington, D.C.: World Bank, 1979.

Yemen Arab Republic. Mashrau: al-Mithaq al-Watani ("Program: The National Charter"). Sanaa, 1980.

Yemen Arab Republic. Thamaniah Ashar min Omar al-Thawra ("Eighteen Years in the Life of the Revolution"). Sanaa: Ministry of Information and Culture, 1980.

Yemen Central Bank. 1981.

Yemen Communique. Legation of the Mutawakkilite Kingdom of Yemen, Washington, D.C., December 1962-January 1969.

Yemen Highway Authority Report on Transportation Development. Sanaa: Yemen Highway Authority, 1981.

Zabarah, Ahmad. Personal interviews. Washington, D.C., 1975 and 1976.

GENERAL WORKS

Arabic

al-Abbasi, Ali ibn Mohammed Abeed. Sirat al-Hadi ila al-Hag: Yahya ibn al-Hussein ("The Biography of the Guide to the Right: Yahya ibn al-Hussain"). Edited by Sahil Zakkar. Damascus: Daar al-Fikr, 1972.

Aflag, Michael. al-Ba'ath wa-al-Ishtirakiah ("Ba'ath and Social-ism"). Damascus: al-Mu'assasah al-Arabiah li'Iddirasat wa al-Nashr, 1950.

al-Attar, Mohammed Said. al-Takhaluf al-Igtisadi wa al-Ijtima'i fi al-Yaman ("The Economic and Social Backwardness in Yemen"). Beirute: Daar al-Dali'ah, 1967.

Awbali, Mohammed H. A. I'ghtial Braitania li-Aden wa al-Janoob al-Arabi: Watha'eg wa Masader ("Britain's Deception of Aden and South Arabia: Documents and Facts"). Beirute: Manshura al-A'asr al-Hadith, 1971.

al-Barrawi, Rashid. al-Yaman wa al-Ingilab al-Akhir ("Yemen and the Latest Revolution"). Cairo: Maktabat al-Nuhdhah al-Musri'ah, 1948.

al-Haddah, Mohammed Y. Ta'rikh al-Yaman al-Siyassi ("The Political History of Yemen"). Cairo: Daar Wahdan lil-Taba'ah wa al-Mashr, 1968.

al-Jirafi, Abdul Allah A. al-Mugtadif min Ta'rikh al-Yaman ("Excerpts from the History of Yemen"). Cairo: Daar Ahya'e al-Kutub al-Arabiah, 1955.

Johar, Hassan M. al-Yaman. Cairo: al-Gowmiah lil-Tarbi'ah wa al-Nashr, 1965.

Muftah, Abdullah ibn. Sharh al-Azhar ("The Elucidation of the Flowers"). Cairo: Mtba'at al-Ma'bad, 1921.

Numan, Mohammed Ahmad. al-Atraf al-Ma'niah ("The Considered Parties"). Aden: al-Sabban wa Shuraka'hu, 1965.

Omar, Sultan A. Nadhrah fi Tagadum al-Mujtama' al-Yamani ("A View into the Social Progress in Yemen"). Beirute: Daar al-Ta'liah lil-Ta'ave'ah wa al-Nashr, 1970.

al-Rayhani, Amin. Muluk al-Arab ("The Arab Kings"). Beirute: Daar al-Rayhani, 1960.

Sa'id, Amin. al-Yaman. Cairo: Daar Ahya al-Kutub al-Arabiah, 1960.

al-Shamahi, Abdullah. Yaman: al-Insan wa al-Hadharah ("Yemen: Man and Civilization"). Yemen: Daar al-Hann lil-Taba'ah, 1972.

Shami, Ahmad Muhammed. Ahmad Hamid al-Din. Beirute: Daar al-Kitab al-Jadid, 1965.

_____. Min al-Adab al-Yamani ("From the Literature of Yemen"). Beirute: Marba'at al-Shuruqu, 1974.

Sharaf al-Din, Ahmad. al-Yaman abr al-Ta'rikh ("Yemen in History"). Cairo: Matba'at al-Sunnah al-Madaniah Abedine, 1963.

al-Thawr, Ahmad, M. Hadhihi hi'a al-Yaman ("This is Yemen"). Sanaa: Matba'at al-Madani, 1969.

al-Wazir, Ibrahim Ali. Bain Yadai al-Ma'sah: Hadith ila al-Yamani'in al-Nazihih ("Between the Hands of Dilemma: A Discourse to the Yemeni Emigrants"). Beirute: Daar al-Tiba'ah wa al-Nashr, 1963.

al-Wazir, Zaid Ali. Muhawalt li-Fahm al-Mashkelah al-Yamaniah
("An Attempt to Understand the Yemeni Problem"). Beirute:
al-Sharikah al-Muttahedah lil-Towze'e, 1968.

Zabarah, Mohammed ibn Mohammed. A'imat al-Yaman ("The
Yemeni Imams"). Taiz: Matba'at al-Nasr al-Naseriya, 1952.

az-Zarkali, Khari-din. Shibhal Jazirah fi Ahad al-Malik Abdul
Aziz ("Portrait of the Peninsula During the Time of King
Abdul Aziz"). Beirute: Matabe Dar al-Galum, 1970.

English

Adams, Arthur E., ed. Soviet Foreign Policy. Boston: D. C.
Heath, 1961.

Almond, Gabriel A., and James S. Coleman, eds. The Politics
of the Developing Areas. Princeton: Princeton University
Press, 1960.

Almond, Gabriel A., and G. Bingham Powell, Jr. Comparative
Politics: A Developmental Approach. Boston: Little Brown,
1966.

Apter, David. The Politics of Modernization. Chicago: University of Chicago Press, 1965.

Azzam, Abd al-Raman. The Eternal Message of Mohammed. New
York: Devin-Adair, 1964.

Badeau, John S. The American Approach to the Arab World.
New York: Harper & Row, 1968.

Bazzaz, A. On Arab Nationalism. London: Stephen Austin, 1965.

Berger, Monroe. The Arab World Today. New York: Doubleday,
1964.

Berque, Jacques. The Arabs: Their History and Future.
London: Faber and Faber, 1964.

Bethman, Eric W. Yemen on the Threshold. Washington:
American Friends of the Middle East, 1960.

Binder, Leonard. Ideological Revolutions in the Middle East. New York: John Wiley, 1964.

____. The Middle East Crisis: Background and Issues. Chicago: University of Chicago Press, 1967.

Boals, Kathryn. Modernization and Intervention: Yemen as a Theoretical Case Study. Ph.D. dissertation, Princeton University, 1970.

Campbell, John C. Defense of the Middle East. New York: Praeger, 1960.

____. The Middle East in the Muted Cold War. Denver: University of Denver Press, 1964.

Copeland, Miles. The Game of Nations: The Amorality of Power Politics. New York: Simon and Schuster, 1969.

Cortada, James N. The Yemen Crisis. Los Angeles: University of California Press, 1965.

Deutsch, Karl. Politics and Government: How People Decide Their Fate. Boston: Houghton Mifflin, 1970.

Eddin, Mohammed M. H. Shehab. Pan-Arabism and the Islamic Tradition. Ph.D. dissertation, American University, Washington, D.C., 1966.

Faroughy, A. Introducing Yemen. New York: Orientalia, 1947.

Finkle, John L., and Richard W. Gable. Political Development and Social Change. New York: John Wiley, 1971.

Fisher, Sidney N. The Middle East: A History. New York: Knopf, 1959.

____, ed. The Military in the Middle East. Columbus: Ohio State University Press, 1963.

Friedrich, Carl J. Man and His Government: An Empirical Theory of Politics. New York: McGraw-Hill, 1963.

de Gauny, Gerald. Faisal. New York: Praeger, 1967.

Gibbons, Scott. The Conspirators. London: Howard Baker, 1968.

Haddad, George. Revolution and Military Rule in the Middle
East: The Arab States; Part II: Egypt, the Sudan, Yemen,
and Libya, vol. 3. Santa Barbara: University of California
Press, 1973.

Halpern, Manfred. The Politics of Social Change in The Middle
East and North Africa. Princeton: Princeton University
Press, 1963.

Heyworth-Dunne, James. al-Yemen: A General Social, Political
and Economic Survey. Cairo: Renaissance, 1952.

Hodgkin, D. C. The Arabs. London: Oxford University Press,
1966.

Ingrams, Harold. The Yemen: Imams, Rulers, and Revolutions.
London: 1963.

Jacob, Harold Fenton. The Kingdom of Yemen: Its Place in the
Comity of Nations. London: 1933.

Karpat, Kemal H., ed. Political and Social Thought in the
Contemporary Middle East. New York: Praeger, 1968.

Keddi, Nikki R. An Islamic Response to Imperialism. Berkeley:
University of California Press, 1968.

Kerr, Malcolm. The Arab Cold War: 1958-1967, 2nd ed.
London: Oxford University Press, 1967.

____. The Middle East Conflict. New York: Foreign Policy
Association, 1968.

Khadduri, Majid. Arab Contemporaries: The Role of Personalities
in Politics. Baltimore: Johns Hopkins University Press, 1973.

____. The Political Trends in the Arab World. Baltimore: Johns
Hopkins University Press, 1970.

Khouri, Fred J. The Arab-Israeli Dilemma. Syracuse:
Syracuse University Press, 1968.

King, Gilliam. Imperial Outpost: Aden. London: Oxford University Press, 1964.

Laqueur, Walter Z. The Middle East in Transition. New York: Praeger, 1958.

Lederer, Ivo. J., and Wayne Vucinich, eds. The Soviet Union and the Middle East. Stanford: Stanford University Press, 1974.

Leibenstein, Harvey. Backwardness and Economic Growth. New York: John Wiley, 1957.

Lenczowski, George. The Middle East in World Affairs. Ithaca: Cornell University Press, 1962.

Lerche, Charles O., Jr., and Abdul A. Said. Concepts of International Politics, 2nd ed. Englewood Cliffs, N.J.: Prentice-Hall, 1970.

Lerner, Daniel. The Passing of Traditional Societies. Glencoe, Ill.: Free Press, 1958.

Lewis, Bernard. The Arabs in History. London: Hutchinson, 1954.

Little, Tom. South Arabia. New York: Praeger, 1968.

Luqman, Farouk M. Yemen 1970. Aden: 1970.

Luqman, Hamed M. The Yemenite Revolution of 1948. Cairo: 1949.

MacDonald, Kenneth W. The League of Arab States. Princeton: Princeton University Press, 1965.

Macro, Eric. Yemen and the Western World Since 1957. London: Hurst, 1968.

Micaud, Charles A. Tunisia: The Politics of Modernization. London: Praeger, 1964.

Nutting, Anthony. The Arabs. New York: Clarkson N. Potter, 1964.

O'Ballance, Edgar. The War in Yemen. Hamden, Conn.: Archon, 1971.

Page, Stephen. USSR and Arabia. London: Central Asian
Research Center, 1971.

Raihani, Ameen. Arabian Peak and Desert: Travels in al-Yaman.
London: Constable, 1930.

Reilly, Bernard. Aden and the Yemen. London: Her Majesty's
Stationary Office, 1960.

Rossi, Mario. The Third World. New York: Funk and Wagnals,
1963.

Sanger, Richard. The Arabian Peninsula. Ithaca: Cornell
University Press, 1954.

Sayegh, Fayez A. Arab Unity: Hope and Fulfillment. New York:
Devin-Adair, 1958.

Schmidt, Dana Adams. Yemen: The Unknown War. New York:
Holt, Rinehart & Winston, 1968.

Shahari, Mohammed A. The Road of the Yemeni Revolution.
Joint Publication Service, 1967.

Sharabi, Hisham. Nationalism and Revolution in the Arab World.
New York: Van Nostrand, 1966.

Sommerville-Large, Peter. Tribes and Tribulations. London:
Robert Hale, 1967.

Spencer, William. Political Evolution in the Middle East.
Philadelphia: J. B. Lippincott, 1962.

Stocking, George W. Middle East Oil: A Study in Political and
Economic Controversy. Nashville: Vanderbilt University
Press, 1970.

Stookey, Robert. Political Change in Yemen: A Study of Values
and Legitimacy. Ph.D. dissertation, University of Texas at
Austin, 1972.

Trelton, Arthur S. The Rise of the Imams in Sana. London:
H. Milford, Oxford University Press, 1925.

Trevaskis, Sir Kennedy. Shades of Amber. London: Hutchinson,
1968.

Vatikiotis, P. J. Conflict in the Middle East. London: George Allen and Unwin, 1971.

Veirer, Jacob. International Track and Economic Development. Oxford: Clarendon Press, 1955.

Walz, Jay. The Middle East. New York: Atheneum, 1965.

Wenner, Manfred. Modern Yemen: 1918-1966. Baltimore: Johns Hopkins University Press, 1967.

ARTICLES AND PERIODICALS

"Aden Two Years Ago." The Economist, February 26, 1966, p. 79.

Ahkaryov, Y. "Arabia and the Yemeni Revolution." New Times, December 5, 1962, pp. 7-8.

"The Arab Middle Class Protests." Atlas (February 1964):109-11.

Badeau, John S. "USA and UAR." Foreign Affairs 43 (January 1965):281-96.

Boutros-Ghali, B. Y. "The Arab League: 1945-1955." International Conciliation. No. 498. (May 1954).

Brown, William. "The Yemeni Dilemma." Middle East Journal 17 (Autumn 1963):349-67.

Dawisha, A. I. "Intervention in Yemen: An Analysis of Egyptian Perceptions and Policies." Middle East Journal 29 (Winter 1975):47-63.

"Egypt's Lame Duck." The Economist, September 24, 1966, pp. 1234-37.

Elis, Spiro. "Dead King Has Plan to Return to Palace." Washington Post, November 11, 1962, p. A-20.

Gibb, Hamilton A. R. "Social Reform: Factor X." Perspective of the Arab World, an Atlantic Monthly Supplement (1956): 17-21.

Guldescu, Stanko, "The Background of the Yemeni Revolution of 1962." Dalhousie Review 45 (Spring 1965):66-77.

____. "The Jeddah Agreement and the Haradh Conference and the Situation in Yemen." World Justice 8 (March 1967):33-40.

____. "War and Peace in Yemen." Queen's Quarterly 74 (Autumn 1967):472-88.

____. "Yemen: The War and the Haradh Conference." Review of Politics 28 (July 1966):319-31.

Halpern, Manfred. "A Redefinition of the Revolutionary Situation." Journal of International Affairs 23 (1969):54-75.

Harbinson, Frederick. "Two Centers of Arab Power." Foreign Affairs 37 (July 1959):672-83.

Hay, Robert. "Great Britain's Relations with Yemen and Oman." Middle East Journal 11 (May 1960):142-49.

Heyworth-Dunne, James. "The Yemen." Middle East Affairs 9 (Fall 1958):50-58.

Holden, David. "At Cross-Purposes in the Sands of Yemen." The Reporter, February 14, 1963, pp. 37-41.

al-Iryani, Abdul Karim. "al-Tanmiah al-Igtissadiah wa al-Khiddah al-Khamsiah fi al-Gomhoriah al-Arabiah al-Yamaniah: Dirassah Tahliliah" (Economic Growth and the First Five-Year Plan in the Yemen Arab Republic: An Analytical Study). Journal of the Gulf and Arabian Peninsula 11 (April 1980):85-111.

Ismael, Tarequ Y. "The Rejection of Western Models of Government in the Arab World: The Case of Nasserism." University of Calgary, Calgary, Canada. Delivered at the 1975 annual meeting of the American Political Science Association, San Francisco, September 2-5, 1975.

Kapil, Menaheim. "Yemen Struggles for Progress." New Outlook I (November/December 1957):34-39.

Kenny, L. M. "Sati al-Husri's Views on Arab Nationalism." Middle East Journal 18 (Summer 1963):231-56.

Kerr, Malcolm. "Coming to Terms with Nasser." International Affairs 42 (January 2967):65-84.

Klieman, Aaron S. "Bab al-Mandab: The Red Sea in Transition." Orbis 11 (Fall 1967):758-71.

Lenczowski, George. "The Objects and Methods of Nasserism." Journal of International Affairs 19 (November 1965):63-76.

Lewis, Bernard. "The Great Powers, the Arabs, and the Israelis." Foreign Affairs 47 (July 1969):642-52.

Macro, Eric. "Yemen: A Brief Survey." Royal Central Asian Social Journal 36 (January 1949):42-53.

Morton, Philip. "Our Yemeni Policy: Pursuit of a Mirage." The Reporter, October 24, 1963, pp. 28-35.

"On Their Heads—And Fighting." The Economist, December 16, 1967, p. 1135.

"Over Their Heads." The Economist, October 14, 1967, p. 145.

Rawling, H. E. "The Aden Cloud Over the Middle East." Contemporary Review 211 (July 1967):22-25.

Rose el-Youssef, January 22-August 22, 1962.

Roucek, J. S. "Yemen in Geopolitics." Contemporary Review 202 (December 1962):310-17.

____. "Yemen in Global Geopolitics." United Asia 18 (May/June 1966):143-51.

Sergeant, R. B. "The Two Yemens: Historical Perspectives and Present Attitude." Asian Affairs 9 (Fall 1973):3-16.

Sharabi, Hisham. "Islam and Modernization in the Arab World." Journal of International Affairs 19 (November 1965):16-26.

____. "Power and Leadership in the Arab World." Orbis (Fall 1963):583-95.

____. "Transformation of Ideology in the Arab World." Middle East Journal 19 (Autumn 1965):471-86.

Voche, H. "What Goes on in Yemen." Atlas (May 1967):21-25.

Whitehead, Philip. "Deadlock in the Yemen." Venture (December 1966):17-22.

Wriggins, Howard. "Political Outcomes of Foreign Assistance: Influence, Involvement, or Intervention." Journal of International Affairs 22 (1968):217-30.

INDEX

ABOUT THE AUTHOR

MOHAMMED AHMAD ZABARAH, a native of the Yemen Arab Republic, teaches at Sanaa University and chairs its Political Science Department.   From 1976 until 1979, he taught at King Abdul Aziz University in Jeddah, Saudi Arabia.   Zabarah received his B.A. from Milton College, his M.A. from Eastern Illinois University, and his Ph.D. from Howard University.

Zabarah is coauthor of two books: <u>Contemporary Scientific Methodology</u> (in Arabic) and <u>Public Administration in Implementation and Organization</u> (in Arabic).   He has also contributed articles, both in Arabic and in English, to a number of periodicals.